Billy Wilder

Billy Wilder

Billy Wilder

Updated Edition

BERNARD F. DICK

New York

Da Capo Press

Library of Congress Cataloging in Publication Data

Dick, Bernard F.
 Billy Wilder / Bernard F. Dick.—Updated ed.
  p.   cm.
 Filmography: p.
 Includes bibliographical references and index.
 ISBN 0-306-80729-7 (alk. paper)
  1. Wilder, Billy, 1906–   —Criticism and interpretation. I. Title.
PN1998.3.W56D53 1996
791.43′0233′092—dc20   96-17793
                                                                  CIP

First Da Capo Press edition 1996

This Da Capo Press paperback edition of *Billy Wilder* is a republication
of the edition first published in Boston in 1980, without the original
"Editor's Foreword," and with the addition of a new afterword,
a new "About the Author," and updates to the chronology and
filmography. It is reprinted by arrangement with the author.

Published by Da Capo Press, Inc.
A Subsidiary of Plenum Publishing Corporation
233 Spring Street, New York, N.Y. 10013

Manufactured in the United States of America

Contents

About the Author

BERNARD F. DICK was born in Scranton, Pennsylvania. He holds a B.A. in Classics from the University of Scranton and a Ph.D. in Classics from Fordham University. He has taught at the College of New Rochelle, Manhattan College, the New School, and Iona College where he chaired the Classics Department from 1967 to 1970. Since 1970, he has been at Fairleigh Dickinson University (Teaneck Campus) where he is presently Director of the School of Communication Arts.

His books include *William Golding* (1967, revised 1987), *The Hellenism of Mary Renault* (1972), *The Apostate Angel: A Critical Study of Gore Vidal* (1974), *Anatomy of Film* (1978, revised 1989), *Billy Wilder* (1980), *Hellman in Hollywood* (1982), *Joseph L. Mankiewicz* (1983), *The Star-Spangled Screen: The American World War II Film* (1985), *Radical Innocence: A Critical Study of the Hollywood Ten* (1989), *Columbia Pictures: Portrait of a Studio* (1991), and *The Merchant Prince of Poverty Row: Harry Cohn of Columbia Pictures* (1993). He also edited the screenplay of *Dark Victory* (1981) for the Wisconsin/Warner Brothers Screenplay Series and has recently completed a history of Universal Pictures, *Universal Pictures: Yesterday, Today, and Tomorrow.*

His monograph on Lillian Hellman appears in supplement 1 of *Scribner's American Writers* (1978). His essays, articles, and reviews have appeared in *Saturday Review, Georgia Review,*

Colorado Quarterly, Literature/Film Quarterly, Comparative Literature, and *World Literature Today.* He has presented papers at meetings of the Modern Language Association, the Society for Cinema Studies, the American Comparative Literature Association, and the Popular Culture Association.

He is married to Katherine M. Restaino, Dean of St. Peter's College at Englewood Cliffs, New Jersey.

Preface

LONGEVITY IN ITSELF does not justify a critical study; but when longevity is combined with genius, it does. In 1979, Billy Wilder celebrated the fiftieth anniversary of a career that began in Berlin, where, in 1929, he wrote—or collaborated on—the script of the legendary *Menschen am Sonntag* (*People on Sunday*). Although his exact contribution to *Menschen am Sonntag* is uncertain, his contribution to world film is not. Wilder is a seven-time Academy Award winner; he has been honored with retrospectives at Cork, Berlin, Cannes, the Museum of Modern Art, and the Los Angeles County Museum of Art; he has been the subject of a biography, several monographs, articles, and doctoral dissertations.

However, like his most famous creation, Norma Desmond of *Sunset Boulevard*, Wilder also experienced a period of decline and rejection—a decade (1964–74) of critical and popular indifference; the humiliation of seeing every major studio in Hollywood turn down *Fedora* in 1977. Yet he has survived; few directors have been able to make their twenty-fifth film in their mid-seventies. Wilder's is more than a career; it is a microcosm of the American film—from the malts and milkshakes of *The Major and the Minor* to the bracing brew of *Fedora*.

In so long a career, there are bound to be failures; Wilder has certainly had some. Wilder's failures are to his body of films what plays like *Period of Adjustment* and *Vieux Carre* are to Tennessee Williams's *oeuvre*—works whose flaws merit discussion because of what they reveal about the author. This study includes a discussion of every film Wilder has directed—the outstanding, the good, and the indifferent. Wilder has never made a really bad film any more than Tennessee Williams has written a really bad play. Like any artist, Wilder overreaches and underestimates.

Many of Wilder's films are adaptations of Broadway hits (e.g., *Sabrina, The Seven Year Itch, Witness for the Prosecution*) as well as of obscure short stories and minor plays (e.g., *The Major and the Minor, Kiss Me, Stupid*). To illustrate Wilder's techniques of adaptation, this study will treat Wilder's sources and analyze the changes—some of them quite radical—that he made in bringing literary material to the screen.

A Wilder film is a visually faithful rendition of the screenplay, a correlation of word and image. This seamlessness is ironic because, except for *The Front Page* and *Avanti!*, there was never a finished script on the first day of shooting; usually, a Wilder script is only two-thirds complete when the filming starts. Some of Wilder's scripts have been published, but the bulk of them have not. Quoting from published screenplays is often misleading because sometimes there is a great difference between the dialogue one reads in the screenplay and the dialogue one hears on the screen. Unless specified, all quotations from the films derive from the films themselves; hence, the punctuation is approximate.

Despite Wilder's predilection for a strong script, he is essentially a filmmaker—a storyteller who relies not only on words but also on images. Thus each film is discussed visually. Film terminology can be abstruse, but for the sake of simplicity, only the following terms will be used: pan shot (horizontal movement—right to left, left to right); tilt shot (vertical movement—up-down, down-up); swish pan (unusually rapid panning that creates a momentary blur); tracking shot (camera placed on moving vehicle or mounted on dolly tracks, moving in and out of a scene); high angle shot (camera above subject at a downward angle); low angle shot (camera below subject, pointed upward); fade out (screen goes black); fade in (scene emerges from blackness); dissolve (a linking of shots as one fades out at the same time that the other fades in).

Wilder has always felt insecure about his English; in fact, he speaks like a *Herr Professor* at a German university—precisely, sometimes pedantically. Thus he has always worked with a collaborator, his two most famous colleagues being Charles

Brackett and I. A. L. Diamond. This study does not purport to answer the question of who contributes what to a Billy Wilder movie. One can say, however, that Wilder's collaborators fared better with him than without him. Wilder could—and did—work apart from Brackett, and although he has been collaborating with Diamond since 1957, he did write the script for *Witness for the Prosecution* (1958) with Harry Kurnitz. On the other hand, when Brackett worked with other screenwriters, the results were forgettable films such as *The Mating Season, Titanic, The Girl in the Red Velvet Swing,* and *Journey to the Center of the Earth.* Before he teamed up with Wilder, Diamond was collaborating on the scripts of such Warner Bros. dreck as *Two Guys from Milwaukee* and *Two Guys from Texas*; since 1957, Diamond worked apart from Wilder on *Merry Andrew* and *Cactus Flower,* neither of which was especially memorable. *QED.*

Finally, while the purists may object, Wilder's eighth film will be referred to as *The Big Carnival,* although its original title was *Ace in the Hole.* In film rental catalogs and television program listings, the film appears under the changed title, which, actually, is more fitting, evoking as it does scorching melodramas like *The Big Sleep* and *The Big Heat.*

There is no difference between the title of this volume and the one to whom it is dedicated.

Acknowledgments

GRATITUDE IS always in order, first to my wife, Katherine Restaino, for spending her vacation with me, sorting through Wilderiana at the Margaret Herrick Library of the Academy of Motion Picture Arts and Sciences in Los Angeles; also, to head librarian, Terry T. Roach, and the staff at that remarkable institution where film research is regarded as scholarship—which is as it should be; to Barbara Humphrys and her magnificent staff in the Motion Picture Section of the Library of Congress, where I was able to view some Wilder films without distraction; to my former student, Martin Nocente, whose knowledge of film puts some of his elders to shame; to Audrey Rubin, Assistant Director of the Fairleigh Dickinson University Library (Teaneck-Hackensack Campus), for obtaining a copy for me of the short story that served as the basis of *The Major and the Minor*; to my colleague Vernon Schonert for providing me with program notes on some of Wilder's German films; to Ted Chesler, Chairman of the Communications Department at Fairleigh Dickinson University (Teaneck-Hackensack Campus), for encouraging me to include Wilder's films in my courses; and to Steve Seidman, whose *The Film Career of Billy Wilder* proved enormously helpful in my own work. Stills are courtesy of the Margaret Herrick Library, Billy Wilder, the Museum of Modern Art/Film Stills Archive, and Movie Star News.

Chronology

1906   Billy Wilder born Samuel Wilder in Sucha, in Polish Galicia (100 miles east of Vienna), on June 22.

1914   Family moves to Vienna at outbreak of World War I.

1924   Enrolls at University of Vienna, leaving after three months; begins writing for *Die Stunde* (The Hour), a Viennese tabloid; specializes in crime features, sportswriting, and interviews.

1926   Leaves Vienna for Berlin as press agent–interpreter for Paul Whiteman; begins writing for Berlin tabloids, earning reputation as crime reporter.

1929   Writes or collaborates on script of *Menschen am Sonntag* (People on Sunday).

1929–   Associated with at least twelve German films for which he
1933   receives story, screenplay, or coscreenplay credit; writes about 200 scenarios for German films without screen credit.

1933   Rise of Hitler causes Wilder to leave Berlin for Paris; codirects *Mauvaise Graine* (The Bad Seed) in Paris; Twentieth Century–Fox remakes his *Ihre Hoheit Befiehlt* (Her Majesty Requests) as *Adorable* for Janet Gaynor, giving Wilder story credit; Universal remakes *Was Frauen Träumen* (What Women Dream), a Wilder coscreenplay, as *One Exciting Adventure*, with Binnie Barnes.

1934   *Pam-Pam*, a script that was never filmed, brings Wilder to attention of Columbia Pictures; arrives in Hollywood; coscreenplay credit for *Music in the Air* (Twentieth Century–Fox).

1935 Coscreenplay credit for *Lottery Lover* (Fox).

1936 Marries Judith Iribe.

1937 Sells *Champagne Waltz* to Paramount but only receives story credit; begins a seventeen-year association with Paramount.

1938 Teams up with Charles Brackett for screenplay of Lubitsch's *Bluebeard's Eighth Wife*; beginning of Brackett-Wilder collaboration; Lubitsch leaves Paramount.

1939 Becomes American citizen; Brackett-Wilder screenplays for *What a Life, Midnight,* and *Ninotchka*; birth of daughter, Victoria.

1940 Brackett-Wilder screenplay of *Arise My Love*; costory credit for *Rhythm on the River.*

1941 Brackett-Wilder screenplays for *Hold Back the Dawn* and *Ball of Fire.*

1942 Directorial debut with *The Major and the Minor.*

1943 *Five Graves to Cairo* (director and coscreenplay).

1944 *Double Indemnity* (director and coscreenplay).

1945 *The Lost Weekend* (director and coscreenplay); heads film unit of American Information Control Division in Germany (May-September).

1946 *The Lost Weekend* wins Academy Awards in categories of Director, Screenplay, and Best Actor.

1947 Wilders divorce.

1948 *The Emperor Waltz* (director and coscreenplay); RKO remakes *Ball of Fire* as *A Song Is Born,* with Wilder receiving costory and coscreenplay credit.

1949 Marries Audrey Young.

1950 *Sunset Boulevard* (director and coscreenplay); end of Brackett-Wilder team.

1951 *Ace in the Hole* (director, costory, coscreenplay, producer); Wilder's debut as producer of his own film; Paramount changes title to *The Big Carnival*; *Sunset Boulevard* wins Academy Awards for Best Story and Screenplay and Art Direction (Black and White).

1953 *Stalag 17* (director, coscreenplay, producer).

1954 *Sabrina* (director, coscreenplay, producer); Wilder leaves Paramount and freelances; William Holden wins Oscar for *Stalag 17.*

1955 *The Seven Year Itch* (director, coscreenplay, coproducer); Wilder's first film in CinemaScope; *Sabrina* wins Academy Award for Edith Head in Best Costume Design (Black and White) category.

1957 *The Spirit of St. Louis* (director and coscreenplay); *Love in the Afternoon* (director, coscreenplay, producer); first collaboration with I. A. L. Diamond.

1958 *Witness for the Prosecution* (director and coscreenplay); publicly expresses interest in producing a Broadway musical about Sherlock Holmes.

1959 *Some Like It Hot* (director, coscreenplay, producer).

1960 *The Apartment* (director, costory, coscreenplay, producer); *Some Like It Hot* wins Academy Award for Orry-Kelly in Best Costume Design (Black and White) category.

1961 *One, Two, Three* (director, coscreenplay, producer); *The Apartment* wins Academy Awards in categories of Best Picture, Director, Writing (Best Story and Screenplay Written Directly for the Screen), Art Direction (Black and White), and Film Editing; Wilder retrospective at Berlin Film Festival in July.

1963 *Irma La Douce* (director, coscreenplay, producer).

1964 *Kiss Me, Stupid* (director, coscreenplay, producer) opens to critical pans and moral indignation; Wilder retrospective at New York Museum of Modern Art in December; Andre Previn wins Academy Award for *Irma La Douce* in Scoring of Music—Adaptation or Treatment—category.

1965 Wilder retrospective at Cork International Film Festival (September).

1966 *The Fortune Cookie* (director, costory, coscreenplay, producer).

1967 Walter Matthau wins Academy Award for Best Supporting Actor in *The Fortune Cookie.*

1969 Charles Brackett dies.

1970 *The Private Life of Sherlock Holmes* (director, costory, coscreenplay, producer).

1972 *Avanti!* (director, coscreenplay, producer).

1973 Signed by Universal to direct *The Front Page.*

1974 *The Front Page* (director, coscreenplay).

1976 Universal buys Thomas Tryon's *Crowned Heads*; Wilder

slated to direct *Fedora*, first of the four novellas in Tryon's book; submits first draft of *Fedora* to Universal, which rejects it.

1977 Leaves Universal; makes *Fedora* with German tax-shelter money.

1978 *Fedora* (director, coscreenplay, producer) screened out of competition at Locarno and Cannes Film Festivals.

1979 Celebrates fiftieth anniversary in films; United Artists releases *Fedora*; a thirty-film Tribute to Billy Wilder at Los Angeles County Museum of Art (July-August).

1981 *Buddy Buddy* (director, coscreenplay)

1982 Tribute from the Film Society of Lincoln Center.

1986 Receives the American Film Institute's fourteenth annual Life Achievement Award.

1988 Receives the 1987 Irving G. Thalberg Memorial Award from the Academy of Motion Pictures Arts and Sciences on Oscar night, 11 April 1988.

1990 Recognized for his contribution to film by the John F. Kennedy Center for the Performing Arts.

1991 Wilder retrospective at New York's Film Forum.

1994 American premiere of Sir Andrew Lloyd Weber's musical *Sunset Boulevard*, "based on the Billy Wilder film."

1995 Presented with the Career Achievement Award by th Writers Guild Foundation.

1

Inside the Spanish Gates: Wilder and Paramount

FIRST WORKS often contain the seeds of greatness, but they rarely bear the fruit of genius. Sometimes those seeds are so microscopic that only a trained eye can discern their presence. One might sense promise in the maiden efforts of D. W. Griffith, John Ford, and Stanley Kubrick; but who could predict on the basis of *The Adventures of Dollie* (1908), *The Tornado* (1917), and *Fear and Desire* (1953) that *The Birth of a Nation* (1915), *The Searchers* (1956), and *A Clockwork Orange* (1971) lay ahead? Similarly, there is little about Billy Wilder's first film, *The Major and the Minor* (1942), to suggest that he would develop into a movie maker with an international reputation. More likely he would become another contract director at Paramount, specializing in films of concealed identity where ladies in disguise and gentlemen with aliases converse in double entendre. One could even imagine Wilder's becoming a screenwriter-director like Preston Sturges but without Sturges's gift of making slapstick respectable. But one would hardly call him Ernst Lubitsch's heir on the basis of *The Major and the Minor.*

Eventually, Wilder would be compared with Lubitsch; but in 1942 Billy Wilder was the other half of "The Happiest Couple in Hollywood," as a *Life* profile dubbed Charles Brackett and himself, at the time the most successful screenwriting team in the industry. For it was not as a director but as a screenwriter that Wilder began his film career; and it was not in Hollywood but in Berlin. Between 1929 and 1933 Wilder was associated with at least twelve German films, although the number was undoubtedly higher.[1] He received story credit for one of them, screenplay credit for two, and coscreenplay credit for the rest.[2] Some of these films are still highly regarded: *Menschen am Sonntag* (People on

23

Sunday, 1929), an idyllic and poignant depiction of two couples on a Sunday afternoon;[3] *Der Teufelsreporter* (The Daredevil Reporter, 1929), a newspaper melodrama reflecting Wilder's own experiences as a reporter in Vienna and Berlin and anticipating his portrayal of the news media in later films such as *The Big Carnival* (1951) and *The Front Page* (1974); and *Emil und die Detektive* (Emil and the Detectives, 1931), a charming "kid sleuth" movie.

When Wilder came to Hollywood early in 1934, it was also as a screenwriter. His first taste of life behind the camera—*Mauvaise Graine* (The Bad Seed, 1933), which he codirected with Alexander Esway in Paris and for which he received story credit—left him eager to return to writing. However, in 1934 the studios were not bidding for Billy Wilder screenplays. Either the scripts were never bought or they were bought and assigned to other screenwriters. Then there were scripts that were sold but never filmed. Finally, one of his screenplays, *Champagne Waltz*, brought him to the attention of a Paramount producer and led to a job as a contract writer. Just as Raoul Walsh is automatically associated with Warner Brothers and Vincente Minnelli with MGM, Billy Wilder is synonymous with the studio on Marathon Street with the famous Spanish gates that Victor Moore guarded in *Star Spangled Rhythm* (1942) and through which Gloria Swanson drove in her Isotta-Fraschini in Wilder's *Sunset Boulevard* (1950); the studio whose logo was a snow-capped mountain within a circle of stars: Paramount.

The View from the Star-Spangled Mountain

While all the studios made essentially the same types of movies in the 1930s and 1940s, each had its specialty. Twentieth Century–Fox was known for its social consciousness films; MGM, for family fare, Universal, for horror, and Republic, for westerns. Paramount's forte was comedy: campus capers during the 1930s with Bing Crosby teaching Music Appreciation 101 to a class of hepcats in *College Humor* (1933); Mae West quadrupling double entendres; Bob Hope, Bing Crosby, and Dorothy Lamour globe-trotting from Singapore to Bali; Betty Hutton ("The Blonde Bombshell") converting her body into a pogo stick; and later Jerry Lewis crossing his eyes until they seemed to converge at his nose. During

the heyday of radio, Paramount showed the face that went with the
voice, introducing radio personalities like Jack Benny, Fred Allen,
and Bob Hope to moviegoers. When Elvis Presley became a
recording and television celebrity, it was Hal B. Wallis at Paramount who groomed him into a movie star. Paramount was the
studio of the people, and no other studio has ever offered the
people so much genuine, unpretentious entertainment.

It was not a literary studio like MGM; Paramount did not adapt
the classics in the grand manner of the leatherbound book that
opened on the screen with cast and credits on vellum and
manicured fingers turning the pages. There was no production
head at Paramount with the creative personality of an Irving
Thalberg or a Darryl F. Zanuck. While Paramount's diffusers
generated the tranquil radiance of sunlight filtered through
latticework, its photography never achieved the translucence of
MGM's or the sharp monochrome of Fox's. Paramount had the
"white look," the creation of German-born art director Hans
Dreier, who, from 1923 to his retirement in 1950, gave Paramount
films their unique visual style: bourgeois bedrooms looked like
incandescent shrines; walls and staircases gleamed like burnished
ivory.[4] Everything shone in the Paramount movies of the 1930s and
1940s, from satin sheets to that indispensable touch of class, the
white telephone.

Ironically, Paramount did not have a fashionable address. It was
not located in Beverly Hills like Fox or in the San Fernando Valley
like Warner Brothers and Universal. The Spanish gates opened
onto Marathon Street in Hollywood itself. Paramount was an
urban studio in the literal sense, but it compensated for its lack of
prestige by cultivating a sense of identity that it promoted as
vigorously as it did its films. Paramount sang the song of the self,
and its gates echoed the refrain. The famous gates were featured in
such Paramount films as *Star Spangled Rhythm, Duffy's Tavern*
(1945), *Variety Girl* (1947), and most memorably in *Sunset
Boulevard*.

Wilder made Paramount the equivalent of a character in the
screenplay he and Brackett wrote for Mitchell Leisen's *Hold Back
the Dawn* (1941); in the film, an alien, played by Charles Boyer,
sneaks onto the Paramount lot where Mitchell Leisen is shooting *I
Wanted Wings*. He proceeds to tell his story to Leisen, who, despite

a busy schedule, lights a cigarette and listens. The alien's story becomes *Hold Back the Dawn*. The movie itself is a strange blend of fact and fiction, with Paramount supplying both and Wilder supervising their amalgamation. Leisen was a contract director at Paramount who really did make *I Wanted Wings* (1941) and for whom Wilder and Brackett wrote three screenplays—*Midnight* (1939), *Arise My Love* (1940), and *Hold Back the Dawn*. Veronica Lake is on the set when the Boyer character arrives; *I Wanted Wings* was her first major film. *Hold Back the Dawn* is pure Hollywood, where myth reverts to history, and history to myth, without violating each other's conventions or the laws of logic.

Although Paramount made serious films such as *Hold Back the Dawn*, its specialty during the 1940s was comedy—sophisticated, topical, farcial, and often interspersed with songs. The form had been established a decade earlier, notably by Ernst Lubitsch, famed for his feather-light touch. The form was operetta, with or without music. Operetta appropriates the conventions of opera—deceptions, disguises, disclosures—and softens them, lightening them musically and inverting them dramatically. An error in love is not the tenor's cue to denounce the soprano but to mask his disillusionment by putting on a virile front. Thus the crushed Count Danilo in Lehar's *The Merry Widow* announces with masculine bravado that he will go to Maxim's and cavort with the ladies; on the other hand, Alfredo in Verdi's opera *La Traviata*, thinking Violetta has returned to her whorish ways, pelts her publicly with banknotes. But there are no whores in operetta; courtesans and women of easy virtue, yes, but no whores. Johann Strauss's *Die Fledermaus* numbers among its characters (1) a bored housewife having an affair with an Italian tenor; (2) her husband, who seduces young girls by dangling a pocket watch in front of them; (3) her maid, who is not beyond turning a few tricks on the side; and (4) a dissolute prince whose parties are meeting places for cheating couples. But in the world of operetta one speaks of flirtation, not adultery; of soubrettes, not sluts; and of masked balls, not swingers' night at the palace.

Operetta was civilized, and it was precisely a civilizing effect that Lubitsch had on Paramount comedy. Lubitsch transformed the sexual merry-go-round into an elegant carousel that moved with music-box delicacy and precision. Lubitsch gave people something better than sex: he gave them sex transfigured; sex as a game with only one rule, decorum. No fleshy bodies intertwined, no messy vestiges of passion, and always a perfectly made bed the next morning. It is also a game that is never resolved; while it seems that the players make love, one never witnesses it. This was the Lubitsch Law of Unfinished Fornication. "Did they or didn't they?" we ask in a Lubitsch film. They did . . . and they didn't. In *Trouble in Paradise* (1932), Lubitsch closes the bedroom door on an amorous couple. Conclusion: they did. In the next scene, they awaken in their respective rooms. Conclusion: they didn't.

In a Lubitsch film, the double entendres fell lightly on the ear; they did not detonate like dirty jokes. In *One Night with You* (1932), a gendarme tells André (Maurice Chevalier) that he cannot make love in the park. André replies that he can make love anywhere, and his companion (Jeanette MacDonald) heartily concurs. In the next scene, André is about to go to bed when he suddenly turns around and faces the camera. "I know what you think," he begins; but then adds that he and the lady are married.

Clearly, Wilder had come to the right studio. Both he and Paramount excelled at films of deception and masquerade that differed from the typical mixup movie in one important way: they were plausible, if not always probable. The characters were sufficiently lifelike to inspire belief. Thus, in *The Major and the Minor*, one could believe a woman would disguise herself as a twelve-year-old to qualify for a half-fare train ticket; one could also accept the consequences of her masquerade. In myth and fairy tale—and the Paramount comedy had elements of both—belief in the protagonist precludes an acceptance of the protagonist's adventures. If one believes in Cinderella, one accepts the glass slipper; if one empathizes with Rapunzel, tower-length hair is not impossible.

Wilder had also come to Paramount at the right time. There was another writer at the studio, a man whose credentials were awesome: Harvard Law School graduate, novelist, and ex-drama critic of the *New Yorker*. Charles Brackett could write fiction and criticism, but the art of screenwriting eluded him. However, he could put his literary gifts at the disposal of someone who knew that screenwriting was the art of thinking visually as well as verbally. Brackett was floundering at Paramount, as was Wilder, whose first year inside the Spanish gates was hardly promising, especially after *Champagne Waltz* had been reassigned to other screenwriters. Either story editor Manny Woolf or producer Arthur Hornblow, Jr. (the accounts vary), got the idea of teaming up Brackett and Wilder, the Republican from Saratoga Springs and the New Dealer from Austria; one with literacy to spare, the other needing it to smooth out his rough English.

Wilder and Brackett first collaborated on the script of Lubitsch's *Bluebeard's Eighth Wife* (1938). Again it seemed that providence was shaping Wilder's career: *Bluebeard's Eighth Wife* marked the end of Lubitsch's tenure at Paramount and the beginning of Wilder's. The film was not vintage Lubitsch, but the plot peg was a Wilder "meet cute" where boy and girl do not just meet; they "meet cute"—in this case, while buying pajamas. The girl prefers the tops; the boy, the bottoms. Long before *The Pajama Game*, Wilder showed that two could sleep as cheaply as one.

Film historians call 1939 the most celebrated year in movie history; it was the year of such classics as *Gone With the Wind, The Wizard of Oz, Mr. Smith Goes to Washington,* and Lubitsch's *Ninotchka,* with script by Brackett, Wilder, and Walter Reisch. Although *Ninotchka* is one of those flawless comedies where performance, production, and script intermingle, one can still see Wilder's touches in this tale of a dour commissar (Greta Garbo) whom love and capitalism transform into a woman. First, there is a printed prologue in the form of a joke that anticipates a similar one in *The Major and the Minor*: "This story takes place in Paris, in those wonderful days when a siren was a brunette, and not an alarm—and when a Frenchman turned off the lights, it wasn't for an air raid"[5] (*Ninotchka*); "The Dutch bought New York from the Indians in 1626 and by May 1941 there wasn't an Indian who regretted it" (*The Major and the Minor*).

Second, the character of Ninotchka fits the image the public had of Greta Garbo as a solitary, aloof, and humorless woman who was actually quite at home in masculine clothes and sensible shoes. As Parker Tyler shrewdly observed, "The movie's plot followed the pattern of her 'private' Hollywood legend of preoccupation and standoffishness."[6] When Ninotchka is asked if she wants to be alone, the audience laughed because Garbo's "I vant to be alone" was as legendary (and apparently as spurious) as Bette Davis's

"Petah" and Cary Grant's "Jeudy." Capitalizing on a star's public image is as much a feature of *Ninotchka* as it is of Wilder's films in general; thus it seems that Wilder was responsible for making the character correspond to Garbo's screen persona. When Wilder was working with a star who was a true screen icon (Marlene Dietrich, Gloria Swanson, Marilyn Monroe), he would incorporate aspects of her mythology into the character she was playing. The classic example is *Sunset Boulevard*, where he made Norma Desmond's life in the film conform to the image a 1950s moviegoer might have of a silent star like Gloria Swanson. Wilder's evocative touches could be nostalgic (Ginger Rogers's dance routine in *The Major and the Minor* that recalled her RKO musicals of the 1930s); amusing (Tom Ewell's joke about having Marilyn Monroe in his apartment in *The Seven Year Itch*); or brutal (Dean Martin playing a lecherous boozer called Dino in *Kiss Me, Stupid*).

In the script for Mitchell Leisen's *Midnight* (1939), Wilder's influence was even more discernible. *Midnight* was a Paramount comedy, while *Ninotchka* was shot at MGM. Studio styles differed; although both *Ninotchka* and *Midnight* were set in Paris, even Lubitsch had to admit that there was a difference between MGM's Paris and Paramount's: "There is Paramount Paris, and Metro Paris, and of course the real Paris. But Paramount's is the most Parisian of all."[7] Wilder was more at home in Paramount's Paris, where the Parisians were more carefree than their Olympian counterparts at MGM.

Midnight was the stuff that screwball comedy is made of. Eve Peabody (Claudette Colbert), an American chorus girl who did not break the bank at Monte Carlo, arrives in Paris with nothing but the gold lamé gown she is wearing. Tibor Czerny (Don Ameche), a cab driver, takes pity on her and even offers to let her stay in his flat while he is out hustling fares. The situation is perfect for Wilder's hidden dialogue where double meanings are grafted on the lines and transmitted vocally (a change of voice, a different inflection) or gesturally (a raised eyebrow, a deadpan look, a double take). Eve is a gold digger, or, less charitably, a floozy. Czerny is too unsophisticated to understand her humor, which is flecked with a breezy cynicism. When he asks her what kind of job she is looking for, Eve replies, "At this time of night, I'm not looking for needlework." Actually, she is looking for a singing job; but the worldly huskiness with which Claudette Colbert delivers the line makes it clear that Eve's skills are not exclusively vocal.

When Eve allows herself to be used by Georges Flamarion (John Barrymore) to break up a romance between Mrs. Flamarion and her lover, she enters Parisian society *à la* Paramount, where adultery is not cheating but *grand amour*, and where homosexuals are fops given to outrageous statements like "Measles can give a child's skin a nice polka dot effect." But *Midnight* is a retelling of *Cinderella*; thus, in discussing it, one uses the idioms of fairy tale, where homosexuals, cuckolds, cheating wives, and gold diggers do not exist except in their higher, euphemistic forms. Furthermore, *Midnight* is a superbly crafted Cinderella story, with everything motivated including Eve's using a pawn ticket as an invitation to a soiree.

Wilder knows exactly how many times he can compound deceptions before they spiral out of control. Czerny shows up at the Flamarions' chateau, where Eve is masquerading as a baroness and attempts to beat her at her own game by pretending to be her husband, the baron. The battle of the sexes becomes a battle of wits; Czerny invents a baby daughter, and Eve retaliates with an insanity charge that brings them to a divorce court to dissolve their nonexistent marriage. The fairy tale starts winding down, but not until history has a chance to make a brief appearance. The year is 1939; at the end of the film, Wilder puts the masquerade into a historical context when the judge reminds Eve and Czerny that, compared to "vast world unrest," their squabbles are insignificant. It is a subtle touch, and one that may even go unnoticed; yet it reveals something about Wilder—his need to give even a screwball comedy a historical framework. Similarly, in the *Ninotchka* prologue, the prewar sirens who pleased the eyes were sadly contrasted with wartime sirens of a different kind that pierced the ears. *Midnight* ends on an upbeat, as a comedy should, but with a gentle admonition that there is a world outside that is less comforting than the powder-puff realm of operetta.

Wilder's most personal script of the 1937–41 period was *Hold Back the Dawn*, which portrayed the plight of an immigrant as only another immigrant could. Wilder had originally written a scene for Charles Boyer, who was playing a Hungarian immigrant, in which the character was so desperate for communication that he talked to a cockroach climbing the wall of his fleabag hotel. When Wilder asked Boyer how he liked the scene, the actor replied that he had it deleted. Boyer refused to talk to a creature that could not answer. It was then that Wilder, who has always been protective of his scripts, realized that if he wanted them to reach the screen intact, he would have to direct them himself.

2

From Wordsmith to Image Maker: *The Major and the Minor*

IN 1941 a studio executive called Wilder's attention to a 1921 *Saturday Evening Post* short story, Fannie Kilbourne's "Sunny Goes Home," in which the title character is a nineteen-year-old actress specializing in children's roles who decides to give up the theater and return to Iowa. Unable to afford the price of a train ticket, Sunny capitalizes on her one talent and passes herself off as a nine-year-old to ride half fare. On board, she meets a man of the world in his late twenties. They are attracted to each other. She reveals her age; he is relieved not to be robbing the cradle; they disembark at South Bend; presumably, they marry.

The story was the basis of a 1923 Broadway flop, Edward Childs Carpenter's *Connie Goes Home*, which enjoyed a run of twenty performances. The title character was now an aspiring actress who came to New York from a home for destitute girls in Illinois. Tired of warding off the advances of wealthy lechers, she also tried to ride for half fare. When a conductor penetrated her disguise, she was befriended by a young man who took her to his uncle's home in Chicago; and, after some complications, took her as his own.

The Major and the Minor (1942)

Could a forgettable short story and a Broadway failure form the basis of a successful movie? Wilder thought so. After badgering Paramount to let him direct a film, he knew he would have to convince the skeptics who were anticipating a pseudo-Lubitsch comedy that was all fluff and frou frou.

After two months of shooting (March-May 1942), Wilder gave Paramount "the most salable hunk of celluloid" he could deliver. He had also divined the public's taste; *The Major and the Minor*

Ginger Rogers disguised as the twelve-year-old Sue-Sue in The Major and the Minor.

was a box-office hit. The film was set in pre–Pearl Harbor America, when the country's innocence was still intact. However, like *Midnight, The Major and the Minor* did not ignore world affairs; it only minimized them. A major, hearing the winds of war, wants active duty; his fiancée wants him safe at a desk; and the minor wants him to serve his country to keep it from going the way of Vichy France. But also like *Midnight,* the contemporary setting is the backdrop for the masquerade. "What did happen to you between New York and Stevenson?" Mrs. Applegate asks her daughter, Susan. "I went to a masquerade," is Susan's reply.

It was more than a masquerade; it was a metamorphosis. Sunny/Connie becomes Susan/Sue-Sue. Tired of giving egg shampoos and massaging scalps, Susan Applegate (Ginger Rogers) decides to leave New York and take the next train to Stevenson, Iowa. When she discovers at the ticket window that she is five dollars short of the fare, Susan ducks into the ladies' room and emerges as Sue-Sue with balloon and lollipop. On board, she is befriended by Major Kirby (Ray Milland), whose fatherly interest in "Sue-Sue" clashes with Susan's womanly interest in him. Inevitably, the minor reveals herself to the major—on a train platform, appropriately enough—where she appears in a tailored suit and picture hat, much to the astonishment of the major, who is so delighted that it never occurs to him that his affection for "Sue-Sue" may not have been especially paternal. Wilder has always prided himself on making a *Lolita* sixteen years before Nabokov's novel. Susan's deception did reveal that Kirby was a bit of a nympholept, to use Nabokov's phrase. But in 1942, nympholepsy was as yet uncoined; Nabokov was lecturing at Wellesley; and Wilder was aiming for a commercial success where the twists were in the plot, not in the psyche.

Adaptation as Renovation

But how can a commercial success come from a Broadway flop which in turn derived from an obscure short story? The answer lies in Wilder's art of adapting for the screen. Wilder does not regard film adaptation as hack work; it is the art of recreating material for another medium. To effect a successful transfer from one medium to another, the adapter must often dismantle the original, sometimes even gut it, until what remains is only what the writer of the original had when he started—the bare foundation. Thus the story and the play provided the foundation: a career woman's disguising herself as a child to travel half fare. But Wilder built his own edifice, decorating it with something that was completely lacking in his sources: wit.

There are probably more memorable lines in Wilder's movies than there are in those of any other filmmaker: "I *am* big; it's the pictures that got smaller" (Gloria Swanson to William Holden in *Sunset Boulevard* when he observes that she was once a big star); "Kneeling bags my nylons" (Jan Sterling to Kirk Douglas in *The Big Carnival* when she explains why she does not pray); "Nobody's perfect" (Joe E. Brown to Jack Lemmon in *Some Like It Hot* when Lemmon pulls off his wig and announces that he is really a male).

For *The Major and the Minor*, Wilder wrote dialogue that ran the gamut from wisecracks and puns ("How do you feel, Sue-Sue?" "So-so.") to double entendre, which can only be effective when the audience wonders if the second meaning were intended, as opposed to knowing that it was. Sometimes Wilder's double entendres are unequivocally dirty, notably in *Irma La Douce* (1963) and *Kiss Me, Stupid* (1964). However, in *The Major and the Minor*, Wilder winks rather than leers, particularly when Major Kirby explains sexual attraction to Sue-Sue in terms of girl as light bulb and boy as moth bumping his wings against it. It is a Lubitsch touch, but *The Major and the Minor* is not a Lubitsch film despite Robert Emmett Dolan's waltzlike score with its variations on "Isn't It Romantic?" We are not inside the world of operetta, only at its gates. Major Kirby is neither a count nor a playboy; Susan is neither a commoner nor a countess in disguise. Her masquerade has been motivated by expediency, not caprice or the urge to trick an unfaithful lover. Kirby and Susan are closer to musical-comedy characters than they are to operetta stereotypes. Thus they are more believable than a couple in a 1930s Lubitsch film, where one cannot tell the waltzer from the waltz.

Since Wilder was trying to give a comic masquerade the semblance of reality, he could not emulate the wedding cake richness of Lubitsch's *The Merry Widow* (1934), nor could he resort to pictorialism and dazzling camera work. However, it would be a mistake to dismiss *The Major and the Minor* as visually uninteresting because it contains no outstanding shots. Wilder has boasted that he never used a phony camera set-up, claiming that the script determines the way the film will be photographed. Wilder approaches directing from a screenwriter's standpoint; thus he is generally able to correlate the visual and the verbal. He also understands the importance of point of view both as a state of consciousness and as the actual perspective from which one sees reality. For example, when Susan discovers she does not have the right fare, Wilder shoots her face from behind the ticket window; Susan is literally behind bars. This may seem a small point, yet the shot conveys her helplessness at being "barred" from returning home. However, when she reappears as Sue-Sue, the shot reflects her point of view; the camera is outside the window. Now it is the ticket seller's face that is barred; he is the one who is helpless because he senses duplicity but cannot prove it.

It is axiomatic that a high angle shot is used when a character is looking down at something. Wilder performs an interesting variation on the high angle shot, investing it with an anticipatory quality. When Pamela, Major Kirby's fiancée, begins to suspect that Sue-Sue is older than she looks, she waits for her to return from a dance. As Susan approaches the house, she is shot from a second-floor bedroom window, where someone is obviously watching. When Susan comes through the front door, an intricate high angle shot makes it clear that someone is spying on her. Susan is photographed through the crack of a bedroom door at the top of the stairs. It was Pamela watching at the window and peering through the crack in the door. Through such shots, Wilder weaves a mood of mystery that culminates in the confrontation between the two women in the dark gymnasium later that evening.

Even in his very first film, Wilder knew how to break a script down into images, repeating an idea visually that had been expressed earlier through dialogue. It would seem that, after Major Kirby's facts-of-life speech, we have heard the last of light bulbs; true, but we have not *seen* the last of them. After Susan returns to Iowa, the camera tracks up to the front porch of the Applegate house. The camera then pans from Mrs. Applegate to Susan's anxious suitor; next, to Susan swinging wistfully in a hammock; and finally, to a light bulb overhead encircled by moths.

An image is indeed worth a hundred words, and the final image is worth a thousand. While waiting for a train, Kirby notices a strikingly dressed woman at the opposite end of the platform who bears an uncanny resemblance to Sue-Sue. When he approaches her, she informs him that she is off to marry a major who will keep America from suffering the fate of Vichy France. Now he knows her identity. As they embrace, they seem to disappear in billows of smoke from the departing train. It is as if one had been witnessing a magic show that ended not with a curtain call, but with the stage engulfed in waves of smoke—a substance as elusive as the art of magic, or the art of moviemaking.

3

Desert Intrigue and Urban Deception: *Five Graves to Cairo* and *Double Indemnity*

WHILE Field Marshal Rommel would seem to have nothing in common with Susan Applegate, Wilder's second film, *Five Graves to Cairo*, was really the reverse of *The Major and the Minor*. The flip side of disguise is deception: a career woman can disguise herself as a child and deceive a major; a British officer can disguise himself as an Alsatian waiter and deceive Rommel. The plot peg of each film was masquerade. Wilder started with a ruse and worked outward, lightening it for comedy, darkening it for melodrama. *Five Graves to Cairo* is a dark masquerade without the high key lighting of *The Major and the Minor*.

Five Graves to Cairo (1943)

Like its predecessor, *Five Graves* was also an adaptation that bore little resemblance to the original; it derives from Lajos Biro's play, *Hotel Imperial*.[1] The play was filmed twice under the title *Hotel Imperial*, once in a 1926 silent version with Pola Negri, and again in 1939 with Isa Miranda. The plot involves an actress who comes to a Balkan border town to investigate her sister's supposed suicide. She takes over her sister's job as chambermaid at the Hotel Imperial; she also falls in love with an Austrian soldier posing as a waiter. When the soldier kills a Russian spy, the actress assumes the blame so he can escape. Just as she is about to be executed, the soldier returns with his troops and rescues her.

Again Wilder gutted the structure and kept the foundation: wartime intrigue in a shabby hotel. First, he changed the time from World War I to World War II; next, he switched the setting from the Balkans to a town on the Libyan border. The mystery of the sister's suicide becomes the mystery of the five graves. Then come

39

the character transformations: the actress becomes Mouche the maid (Anne Baxter), whose concern is not for her dead sister but for her imprisoned brother; the Austrian soldier who disguised himself as a waiter is now a British officer called Bramble (Franchot Tone). The hotel is teeming not with Russians but Nazis, and its most distinguished guest is the Desert Fox himself (Erich von Stroheim). Thus Bramble will kill a Nazi, not a Russian. Mouche covers for Bramble; but this time, unfortunately, there is no last-minute rescue.

Outfoxing the Desert Fox

Five Graves opens strikingly: the credits appear in typescript as if a historical document were about to unfold; a tank moves across the dunes; and a printed prologue specifies the time—June 1942, right after the fall of Tobruk. The tank that was zigzagging across the dunes like a caterpillar now comes into view. A soldier drags himself out of the hatch and collapses on the sand. The camera tracks in for a close-up of his dogtag: Bramble. He crawls across the desert until he stumbles onto the main street of a village. Suffering from sunstroke and delirium, he staggers into the Empress of Britain hotel. The entire sequence is wordless except for Bramble's incoherent muttering; shots dissolve into each other as if melted by the desert heat.

However, once Bramble arrives at the hotel, the plot begins; he will impersonate a crippled waiter who died the night before in an air raid. In Wilder, every incident is a whorl on the narrative wheel. Inevitably, the waiter's body will be discovered, and the masquerade will end; but not before Bramble discovers the secret of the five graves. Yet, for all its air of espionage, the film occasionally veers into comedy; and the occasion is Erich von Stroheim, who plays Rommel as if he had wandered onto the set of *The Merry Widow* and decided to stay. When von Stroheim speaks, the dialogue becomes repartee. At lunch, he looks disdainfully at the dessert: "Rice pudding in Egypt! One never knows if it's raisins or flies." When Mouche tries to charm him into interceding for her brother, Rommel reprimands her for playing the scene badly and advises her to brush up on Italian opera if she wants to be a sacrificial heroine.

Wilder's ability to integrate melodrama, high comedy, suspense, and finally sentiment derives from his talent for connecting plot and subplots by uniting them concentrically or causally. In *The Major and the Minor*, the subplot (Kirby's desire for active service and Pamela's attempts to keep him at the military academy) evolves from the main plot (Susan's masquerade). The masquerade brings Susan and Kirby together and makes it possible for Kirby's ambition to be realized.

Similarly, the secret of the graves is the unifying principle of *Five Graves to Cairo*. Numerical motifs are common in thrillers— e.g., Agatha Christie's *Ten Little Indians*, Dorothy L. Sayers's *The Nine Tailors*, Earl Derr Biggers's *Seven Keys to Baldpate*. In the film, there were five men in the tank, all of whom were killed except Bramble: "Five little Britishers out in the sun/Out hunting Jerries, and then there was one," Bramble muses sardonically. Significantly, Rommel occupies Room 5 in the hotel. And, of course, there is the puzzle of the five graves. An old newspaper clipping about a German archaeologist called Cromstaetter, who came to Egypt on a dig in 1937, is the clue. The archaeologist was none other than Rommel, who was not excavating ruins but digging supply depots between Tobruk and Cairo. Their exact location could only be ascertained from Rommel's map of Egypt, where each of the five letters (E G Y P T) marked the site of a depot.

Since *Five Graves* is a 1943 war movie, one expects that the Nazis will be portrayed unfavorably. They are a swinish lot, double-crossers and born tormentors of women; one of them not only pulls Mouche's apron off and wipes his sweaty face with it, but also tricks her into believing he can effect her brother's release from a concentration camp. Rommel is the exception because he is Erich von Stroheim, who seems to be above everybody and beyond censure. Thus, when he has Mouche brought to trial, one knows it is the Nazis—not Erich von Stroheim—who must be held responsible for her execution.

The ending is one of Wilder's most sentimental; it prefigures the conclusion of *The Private Life of Sherlock Holmes* (1970), where a man also grieves for a woman who has been executed. When Bramble returns to the Empress of Britain several months later, he learns that Mouche lies buried in a nearby cemetery; to help him escape, she paid the ultimate price. Opening the parasol he had brought her as a gift, Bramble places it on her grave and delivers a bitter eulogy. The speech is perfectly motivated; it is not the kind of flag-waving rhetoric designed to send youths marching out of the theater and over to the recruiting office. First of all, Bramble is British; but more important, he is not waving any flag. He is more bitter than patriotic. When he exclaims, "We'll beat the blazes out of them," he is trying to comfort Mouche's spirit and himself as well, since her heroic act earned him a promotion from corporal to lieutenant. The fact that the Nazis were responsible for Mouche's death is not as important as the fact that it must be avenged.

Except for *Ball of Fire* (1941), the Brackett-Wilder scripts of the 1940–43 period were all critical of wartime neutrality. *Arise My Love* ends with the fall of France and a speech that Gusto (Claudette Colbert) delivers to a disillusioned pilot with a broken arm: "My voice is just a little squawk, I know, but I want to use it without somebody's hand over my mouth. And you—what a job you've got! Making tens of thousands of American pilots for tens of thousands of American planes!" There was even a political subtext in *The Major and the Minor*; Susan turned a paper major into a real one and extricated him from the apolitical Pamela, who, had she been living in France, would be giving "beguiling" dinner parties for the Vichyites. In *Five Graves*, Mouche was initially as apathetic as the neutrals in the vestibule of Dante's hell. When she hears that Rommel's troops have arrived, she instinctively puts on some lipstick; her sole concern is her brother. "It isn't one brother that matters; it's a million brothers," Bramble argues. Ironically, his parable of brotherhood made a lasting impression on her.

Double Indemnity (1944)

That *Double Indemnity* should follow *Five Graves* is not surprising; it is a film of double deception and double-crosses. Just as Bramble impersonated a crippled waiter, Walter Neff of *Double Indemnity* must pass himself off as a man with a broken leg on board a train; just as Susan Applegate was almost trapped by a suspicious conductor when she went out on the observation platform for a smoke, Neff is forced into a conversation with a garrulous passenger while trying to keep his face hidden—also on an observation platform.

Five Graves darkened the masquerade; *Double Indemnity* blackened it into *film noir*, that elusive phrase the French coined to describe a type of American melodrama where life is lived amid shadows and fog; where women with a past and men with no future pass their time in sleazy hotel rooms or smoke-filled cocktail lounges. *Film noir* is many things: a murderess in lounging pajamas and a gold ankle bracelet; a car parked by the railroad tracks; a living room in a stucco-front house where a murder is plotted on a summer afternoon; a neon-lit supermarket where an adulteress and her accomplice whisper to each other across a wall of canned goods. However, Wilder did not set out to make a *film noir* any more than Dostoyevsky set out to write existential novels. Wilder, with Raymond Chandler as his collaborator, was simply adapting James Cain's *Double Indemnity* for the screen. It was a difficult task for two reasons: Cain and Chandler.

Like many hardboiled novels, *Double Indemnity* was unfilmable as written. It exuded an air of decay that was more literary than cinematic; the murderess inhabits a "House of Death" with scarlet draperies; she even dresses as Death. Overripeness is all; one keeps thinking of rotting palm trees and clusters of bursting yucca. This time, it was not a question of dismantling the original; it was a matter of stripping away the lurid trappings and retaining the narrative framework: the story of an insurance salesman who conspires with the wife of one of his clients to murder her husband, making it look like a railroad accident so the insurance company would have to pay double indemnity on his policy. The ending, however, would have to go; its perverse romanticism could evoke laughter from a 1940s audience. Cain concludes the novel on board a steamer where the wife, now dressed as Death in a blood-red shroud and whitened face, enters the insurance salesman's stateroom, presumably for the Big Love Death. In 1944, most audiences would not understand anything quite so operatic, but they would understand the wife's plugging the salesman and the salesman's returning the double-cross.

Wilder's second hurdle was Chandler, who, initially, did not understand that Paramount's contract writers worked in an office in the Writers Building, not at home.[2] Wilder needed a true collaborator; he was used to working with Brackett, who would curl up on the sofa and take down Wilder's ideas as he paced up and down, swinging a cane. Although Chandler claimed that working with Wilder probably shortened his life, he was forced to admit that the experience taught him something about screenwriting, as he proved two years later in his original screenplay *The Blue Dahlia* (1946).

As tension-filled as the Chandler-Wilder collaboration must have been, it resulted in one of the most admired screenplays in movie history and one of the few that can be read as literature.[3] But *Double Indemnity* is first and foremost a film; it is from this premise that any discussion must proceed.

The Screenplay Visualized

The credits start with a figure on crutches walking into the frame, blackening it with his shadow. Wilder obviously borrowed the opening from Hitchcock's *Saboteur* (1942), where a menacing shadow grew progressively larger; but Wilder's opening was even more doom-ridden than Hitchcock's. The darkness spreads across the screen, disappearing into the early-morning fog. A car careens along a Los Angeles street; after a series of dissolves, Wilder's favorite way of linking shots, the car pulls up in front of an office building. The driver parks, enters the building, and takes the elevator to the offices of the Pacific All-Risk Insurance Company. He stands on the balcony overlooking rows of desks and filing cabinets, and the camera peers over the railing at the deserted warren. The man goes into his office, inserts a cylinder into the dictaphone, and begins a memorandum to his supervisor in which he confesses to the murder of one of his clients.

Since Walter Neff (Fred MacMurray) is telling his own story, he becomes the film's narrator; and the film takes the form of a flashback, or rather a series of flashbacks, with fluid transitions from past to present. Wilder continually reminds us that Neff is the narrator by returning periodically to Neff at the dictaphone; and every time he does, the bloodstain on Neff's suit jacket gets larger. But no matter how successfully Wilder steered the action between the poles of present and past, even if he surpassed Arthur Miller in *Death of a Salesman, Double Indemnity* would have remained word-locked unless Wilder had been able to make these flashbacks cinematic, not just narrative transitions.

It is difficult to talk about Wilder's visual style because it is so unobtrusive; what interests Wilder is the classic correlation of word and image, of idea and its visualization. For example, when Phyllis Dietrichson (Barbara Stanwyck) comes to Neff's apartment to seduce him into murdering her husband, they embrace on the sofa. "We just sat there," Neff's voice is heard saying as the camera starts tracking back slowly, leaving the couple alone presumably to do more than just 'sit there.' At first, one wonders why—and where—the camera is retreating; but then Wilder dissolves back to Neff at the dictaphone, continuing with his memorandum; after a while, the camera tracks back from Neff, and another dissolve returns us to the apartment as Phyllis is about to leave. The combined tracking shots and dissolves from the apartment to the insurance office and back create fluidity; but they also suggest that a moment of intimacy has taken place to which neither we nor the camera were privy.

The Narrating "I"

Neff's voice bridges the flashbacks, introducing and concluding each of them. The effect, then, is one of first-person narration which, in film, is really voice-over—one of the most abused practices in the media. Unimaginative filmmakers rely on voice-over as a narrative crutch; television debases it by selling products with the voices of unseen celebrities. Although voice-over is presently a cliché, Wilder raised it to the level of classic first-person fiction in *Double Indemnity*.

There is nothing forced about the voice-over in *Double Indemnity* because the film is in the form of an office memo. A memo requires a date, and so Neff supplies one (July 16, 1938); but the memo is also a confession requiring personal details. Neff supplies these as well: age (thirty-five), marital status (single), identifying marks ("no visible scars; not yet, at least"). Wilder has made the opening of the memo a true prologue that gives the audience all the information it needs and in a totally natural way, without cumbersome exposition.

Double Indemnity may be an office memo, but it is one

designed to be seen, not read; and one designed to be seen from a particular point of view—Neff's. Just as Flaubert filtered much of the action of *Madame Bovary* through Emma's consciousness, Wilder also keeps everything pretty much within Neff's range of vision. Thus we not only see what Neff sees; we also see it his way, refracted through the vision of a fast-talking insurance agent with an oil well for a personality.

Neff's manner leaves an oil slick on everything. Therefore, if *Double Indemnity* reeks of sleaze, one must remember that sleaze is characteristic of the narrator. Neff lives in a studio apartment, sparsely furnished and harshly lit; he eats out since his culinary abilities consist of squeezing an occasional grapefruit. Neff spends much of his time on the road; he is a hustler with an enviable sales record because he knows how to talk his way into a house, pushing past the maid to con the mistress. His world is either streaked with shadow or overlit, sinister or garish. Since Neff is our reflector, what we see is characterized by either chiaroscuro or glare. When he enters the Dietrichson house, the walls are flecked with shadows; one has the impression the sun sets in the living room. Conversely, Neff's chintzy apartment has the hard glare of undiffused light.

Neff likes women, but on a purely superficial level; the first thing he notices about Phyllis Dietrichson is her ankle bracelet. Phyllis is the *femme fatale* of detective fiction and *film noir*—the rhinestone tarantula at the center of a spangled web. Wilder makes her a blonde, the avatar of the white goddess. Two years before Tay Garnett dressed Lana Turner in white for the role of Cora in *The Postman Always Rings Twice* (1946), Wilder was exploring the paradoxical connection between white and evil. Unlike Cora, Phyllis does not constantly wear white; but she does in the crucial scenes—her visit to Neff's apartment when she appears in a white cashmere sweater that provocatively reveals the straps of her slip; and the shootout when she is dressed in white lounging pajamas. There are times when Phyllis looks death-white. When she pours out her hatred for her husband in Neff's apartment, the light from a floor lamp washes out her face, leaving it an incandescent mask of loathing.

Phyllis, in fact, makes her first appearance in white. When Neff stops at the Dietrichson house to check on her husband's lapsed

Double Indemnity: Barbara Stanwyck and Fred MacMurray as the unholy pair staging the "accident."

policy, he sees Phyllis at the top of the stairs, her body draped in a white bathtowel. Significantly, Wilder does not show Phyllis in close-up; he uses a low angle shot reflecting Neff's point of view. After all, Neff is in the foyer looking *up* at the white goddess; when Phyllis looks down at him, his diminished size suits the position of a thrall in the goddess's presence.

Because Neff is a man who sees women piecemeal, Phyllis becomes a woman of moments and parts. When she descends the stairs, she is a pair of legs and a gold ankle bracelet. Phyllis is allure alternating with crassness; blonde ice melting into vulnerability. There is one moment, and only one, when Phyllis is fleetingly human; it occurs when she fires at Neff. Phyllis experiences a split second of regret; she admits she is "rotten" and begs Neff to hold her. He does, and Wilder frames the shot so that she is looking into his eyes. Again, we see what Neff sees—a face that, for an instant, loses its rodentlike sharpness and becomes almost human. But it is only for an instant; Neff fires back, killing her. He murdered Phyllis presumably because he knew she had similar plans for him. Yet he fired when Phyllis was most vulnerable: when the goddess had a lapse of divinity. Perhaps Neff had a deeper reason for killing her; perhaps he saw the mortal behind the mask and decided to destroy a myth that could not sustain its mystery.

Fathers and Sons

While the structure of *Double Indemnity* is circular, beginning and ending in the same place, the characterization is triangular: Neff as the base with Phyllis and Keyes as the sides. Barton Keyes (Edward G. Robinson), the claims manager for whom Neff's memo is intended, is as much a part of Neff's life as Phyllis is; in fact, Keyes is even a more important part of it. The only pure relationship in the film exists between these two men. They are surrogate father and son, each possessing what the other lacks— both physically and spiritually. Neff looks up to Keyes because he has integrity; Keyes literally looks up to Neff because Neff is taller than he is. One must remember that everything in the film is seen from Neff's point of view, including physical appearances. When Keyes delivers his speech on the responsibilities of a claims manager, he is pacing in the background, looking like a blustering dwarf. Neff is seated on the desk, left of frame, dominating the shot. Visually, one is getting Neff's view of both himself and his supervisor.

Therefore, Wilder could not photograph Edward G. Robinson in such a way as to minimize his shortness. However, Robinson had an iconic strength that did not reside in his frame; within, there was a metamorphic power that could turn a pudgy man with a snarling mouth into a dynamo who spoke in verbal gunfire. In *Little Caesar* (1931) that power manifested itself as upward mobility spurring Caesar Enrico Bandello to graduate from petty robberies to bank heists; in *Double Indemnity* it appears as a moral force impelling Barton Keyes to prosecute wrongdoers. When Keyes thinks Phyllis may have been responsible for her husband's death, he is determined to expose her. He even has Neff investigated; but since Neff had established an alibi for the night of the murder, Keyes can unearth nothing. Still, the suspicion was there; but it was the paternal kind a father might feel toward a prodigal son, not the vindictive kind a claims manager would feel toward a woman trying to cheat his company.

That Neff loves this man is not surprising; one loves what one lacks. Neff would often end his conversations with Keyes by saying, "I love you, too"; masking his true feelings with a smart-alecky tone of voice. The film ends with the same admission of love, now devoid of glibness. Phyllis's bullet has done its job. Bleeding profusely, Neff comments on the irony of Keyes's looking for a murderer who was so close that he was "right across the desk." Keyes answers, "Closer than that, Walter." Barely able to prop himself against the door, Neff manages to put a cigarette in his mouth but cannot light it; Keyes lights it for him. "I love you, too," Neff says—this time, meaning every word.

In the final scene, Neff reveals something about himself that was not in the memo: a decency that short-circuited. Neff was the victim of the virility myth that reduced him to the stereotype of the bachelor-salesman, posing self-confidently with his hands in his pockets; leering at a woman's anklet; and fancying himself a wit when all he can do is turn a trashy phrase. Keyes was the victim of a similar myth: the myth of the man's man who expresses affection for his own sex in gestures—the handshake, the bear hug, the pat on the back—but never in the idioms of love. The closest Keyes comes to breaking the taboo is by replacing a gesture with a ritual—the lighting of Neff's cigarette—and switching from blunt speech to language of tender ambivalence. Still, better ambivalence than silence.

Oddly enough, *Double Indemnity* was supposed to end with Neff's going to the gas chamber. Wilder disliked the ending; it was exactly what the self-righteous would expect. Despite Chandler's objections, Wilder replaced the gas chamber with one of the most powerful images of male love ever portrayed on the screen: a *pietà* in the form of a surrogate father's lighting the cigarette of his dying surrogate son.

4

Urban Deception and Desert Intrigue: *The Lost Weekend* and *The Big Carnival*

WILDER HAS always been a realistic director, not in the sense that he shows impact wounds and spurting blood, but in the sense that he gives his films a realistic quality by including whatever is dramatically relevant in a particular shot and by correlating camera angle with point of view. If one character is the film's reflector or center of consciousness, Wilder presents the action from that character's perspective. No matter what a Wilder film is about (a middle-aged man's erotic fantasies or Lindbergh's transatlantic flight), it generally has verisimilitude: one believes that what happened on the screen could happen in real life.

Film realism can be achieved in several ways, two of the main ones being on location shooting and *mise-en-scène*. Freely translated, *mise-en-scène* means stage direction; in moviemaking, it means directing a film with the same care and sense of detail that a stage director brings to a play to give as close an approximation of reality as possible. However, in the theater, scenes are played whole; there is no cutting from one character to another; no close-ups, no long shots. A filmmaker, on the other hand, must cut, although realists try to minimize cutting. Some directors—Hitchcock in *Rope* (1948), Miklós Jancsó—have tried ten-minute takes and sequence shots; but the results tended to be static and anticinematic. As a compromise between sequence shots and frequent cutting, realists like Wilder and Renoir prefer the long take—a shot that is temporally longer than the typical shot and, as a result, able to encompass more detail.

Rye and Realism

What makes *The Lost Weekend* (1945) a realistic film is the *mise-en-scène*, not the scenes that were filmed on New York's Third

53

Ray Milland as the deteriorating Don Birnam in The Lost Weekend.

Avenue or even the theme of alcoholism. Because *The Lost Weekend*, which Wilder and Brackett adapted from Charles Jackson's 1944 novel, recounts five days in the life of an alcoholic, some critics have termed it a film of social realism. Yet it is not a movie about alcoholism the way *Smash-Up* (1947), *I'll Cry Tomorrow* (1955), and *Days of Wine and Roses* (1962) are. Don Birnam (Ray Milland) is not a typical movie drunk; he is not the victim of a boyhood trauma, career pressure, or a stormy marriage; he is not grieving for a dead child. Although he never finished college, he is well educated—at times, pretentiously so. He had a story reprinted in *Reader's Digest*; he is a concertgoer and an opera buff. Why, then, does he drink?

In the novel, Jackson implied that part of Don's problem was his expulsion from his college fraternity for writing a love letter to a male student he idolized. However, Wilder had enough problems skirting the Production Code without making Birnam a latent homosexual; yet, curiously enough, Wilder made the male nurse Birnam encounters at Bellevue an offensively obvious faggot. In the movie, Don drinks to forget that he is worse than a failed writer; he is a non-writer whose collected works, apart from his single publication, consist of one-paragraph short stories and opening-scene plays. Sober, Birnam is a nonentity; drunk, he is Shakespeare.

Admittedly, few people can relate to such literary reasons for drinking. Thus what one remembers about the film is not the basis of Birnam's alcoholism, but key scenes such as his hallucination of a bat killing a mouse; and his Third Avenue death march in search of a liquor store open on Yom Kippur. What concerned Wilder was not Don the alcoholic but Don the man—the self-pitying, egocentric, callous heel. Even the opening makes it plain that what is important about the character is not his alcoholism but his duplicity. The camera pans left to right, from the New York skyline to the rear of an East Side apartment house where a liquor bottle, suspended by a rope, is hanging out of one of the windows. Significantly, the camera does not move in for a close-up of the bottle; Wilder, like Flaubert at the beginning of *Madame Bovary*, is moving from the general to the particular; from the milieu to the man. Thus the camera proceeds through the window until it is inside Don Birnam's bedroom, where he is packing for a weekend with his fiancée, Helen (Jane Wyman), and his brother Wick (Phillip Terry).

Reflections in a Glassy Eye

Like *Double Indemnity, The Lost Weekend* is also told from one point of view—Birnam's. Although Birnam is not narrating the film except for two flashbacks, *The Lost Weekend* seems to be a first-person movie because everything is portrayed from one person's perspective. Birnam is a would-be novelist who prefers the solipsistic comfort of drink and self-pity to the rigors of writing. When his eyes are not glazed, they are furtive, distrusting; naturally, they see no beauty. Since he is our reflector, everything looks tawdry, even the Metropolitan Opera House. Birnam is also a sneak; he cannot enter a liquor store without being on the defensive. To convey his feeling of always being spied upon, Wilder shoots him from behind a row of bottles as he enters the store.

At the beginning of the film, Birnam is trying to think of a way to get Helen and Wick out of the apartment so he can get drunk. As he is trying to convince them to use his concert tickets and take a later train to the country, he begins walking into the right of the frame, dominating it and leaving Helen and Wick in the background. The effect is chilling; it is as if Birnam were photographing himself, illustrating the nature of obsession by showing how the obsessed relegates everyone to the background—except himself.

Like Lubitsch, who understood the dramatic use of objects, Wilder makes apartment fixtures and furnishings an integral part of his *mise-en-scène*. He frames shots inside doorways and windows; he uses details of the physical setting for dramatic effect. Birnam hides a bottle in the lighting fixture suspended from the ceiling; Helen realizes that Birnam plans to shoot himself when she sees his revolver reflected in the shaving mirror.

Even the dissolves are from Birnam's point of view; they are a drunk's dissolves, hazy and etherized, accompanied by Miklós Rózsa's otherworldly music that evokes receding consciousness. These dissolves introduce the film's two flashbacks. In the first, Don tells Nat the bartender how he and Helen met three years earlier at a matinee of *La Traviata*. The camera pans right to left;

Birnam's face disappears in a boozy mist as the flashback begins. Although most viewers remember *The Lost Weekend* for the hallucination scene where the mouse and bat replace the proverbial pink elephants, Wilder's real achievement in the film is the opera sequence. During the first-act "Drinking Song," Birnam has an uncontrollable urge for liquor. It is as if the entire cast is conspiring to get him drunk. Violetta and Alfredo toast each other; the guests at the party raise their glasses. The swaying gowns of the choristers dissolve to raincoats swaying on a rack in the coat room. A close-up singles out Birnam's raincoat, and a double exposure reveals the bottle of rye in one of the pockets.

The second flashback in which Birnam panics when he has to meet Helen's parents is also a combination of right-left pan and dissolve—a technique Wilder will repeat in *The Seven Year Itch* (1955). It is an effective device because the flashback becomes an unbroken transition from present to past, from consciousnesss to reverie. The pan moves Birnam out of the present; the dissolve submerges him in the past—namely, the lobby of the hotel where Helen's parents are staying. When Birnam overhears them talking about him, he ducks into a phone booth and has Helen paged. She, of course, does not know Birnam is only at the other end of the lobby. To convey physically what it is like to speak on the phone to someone and watch that person at the same time, Wilder shoots through the glass of the phone booth, from Don in the foreground to Helen across the lobby with her parents in the midground, sitting on a settee.

Everything is shown from Birnam's point of view, including his search for liquor on Yom Kippur. As he walks up Third Avenue, the camera tracks him, sometimes even standing in for him in the form of unsteady movement. When he returns to his apartment, he is so inebriated that he falls down the steps. Wilder uses a subjective shot that just records the sensation of a fall without our ever seeing the person who fell.

Wilder has a fondness for redemptive or sentimental endings that soften the blows of an iron-fisted plot; however, they can only work if the characters are capable of redemption or sentiment, as Bramble and Keyes were in *Five Graves to Cairo* and *Double Indemnity*, respectively. Don Birnam is not such a character. Helen does save him from suicide with a "Write that book" speech which belongs in another movie or at an AA meeting, but her action is not finally redemptive. Don is always threatening to write a novel; he has a title, *The Bottle*; but one wonders if he will ever complete a first chapter. Thus *The Lost Weekend*'s realism is the result of Wilder's *mise-en-scène*, not his portrayal of an alcoholic. Even the ending discourages one from regarding the film as social realism. Now the camera reverses the direction of the opening shot and pans from right to left, away from Birnam's apartment and back to the New York skyline. Birnam's voice accompanies the pan as it asks our sympathy for the "poor bedeviled guys on fire with thirst." The novel ended more honestly—with Birnam as one of the bedeviled.

The Big Carnival (1951)

Seven years after *The Lost Weekend*, Wilder did attempt social realism but failed. The true companion piece of *The Lost Weekend* was a film originally entitled *Ace in the Hole* (1951). It was so badly received that Paramount withdrew it from circulation for a short time and then released it as *The Big Carnival*—"big" being one of those Hollywood adjectives that guaranteed a tough, no-nonsense movie (e.g., *The Big Sleep, The Big Clock, The Big Heat, The Big Steal*).[1]
Throughout the 1940s Wilder had been moving toward a film that would rebut the optimists who believed in man's innate goodness. On the eve of his first decade as a director, which coincided with the rise of McCarthyism, Wilder embarked upon a witch hunt of his own. However, Wilder's witches were not scared movie people who attended the wrong rally or who supported Henry Wallace in 1948. They were Americans who would drive out of their way to visit a carnival; not a church-sponsored carnival but one set up for the crowds that have descended upon an obscure New Mexico trading post whose owner is entombed in a nearby mountain, the victim of a cave-in. No less American is the newspaperman who allowed the victim to remain entombed so he could get a story. A quarter of a century before *Network* (1976) revealed the monsters of the media, Wilder identified those who make the media monstrous: fame-hungry reporters who create news stories to advance their reputations.

The film's point of departure is the case of Floyd Collins, the Kentuckian who, in 1925, was trapped in a cave for eighteen days. But to dispel any notion that the cave-in victim was Collins, Wilder alludes to the Collins case in the script and sets the action in 1950 with references to Yogi Berra, the Broadway musical *South Pacific*, and Lindy's restaurant; he even includes a few snatches from that World War II favorite, "The Hut-Sut Song." Admittedly, *The Big Carnival* is an ugly film; even the credits appear on dirt. Yet what Wilder is illustrating is something that can only be appreciated in retrospect: the connection between failure and corruption.

Chuck Tatum (Kirk Douglas) has been fired from eleven papers before he lands a job with the *Albuquerque Sun-Bulletin*, whose motto is "Tell the Truth," a belief Tatum does not share. A transplanted New Yorker, Tatum is languishing in the desert. He ridicules his colleagues on the paper and tries to impress a cub reporter with his philosophy of journalism: "Bad news sells best because good news is no news."

En route to cover a rattlesnake hunt, Tatum imagines what would happen if fifty rattlers were loose in the city and all but one accounted for. The story could be spread over several days, each installment more dramatic than the next. Finally, Tatum would recover the missing snake which he had in his possession all the time; he would also become a self-created—and self-inflated—popular hero. However, Tatum never gets to the rattlesnake hunt; instead, he picks up a trashy blonde (Jan Sterling) who tells him that her husband, Leo Minosa, is trapped in a cave somewhere in the Mountain of the Seven Vultures. "Forget the rattlesnakes," he tells his editor. "We have birds, vultures."

Wilder, who once worked for a scandal sheet in Vienna, knows the Tatum kind of reporter who first needs a lead and then an angle. Tatum gets his lead when he discovers that Leo feels he has angered the mountain's gods by stealing their burial urns; Tatum also has his headline: "KING TUT IN NEW MEXICO." Leo Minosa is now the mortal of myth, cursed by the gods for pilfering their ancient treasures.

Leo could have been out in sixteen hours if the rescue team had shored up the walls with timber; but Tatum needs a week to publicize the myth he has created. Convincing the local sheriff that

Kirk Douglas digging up a story in *The Big Carnival*

a dramatic rescue would guarantee his reelection, Tatum has the engineers drill from the top of the mountain instead of shoring up the walls and going in after Leo directly. At this point, the film itself moves into myth or rather into a mythic parody; it becomes a transmogrification of the *Book of Genesis* and a travesty of the six days of creation. We are back in the archetypal Garden, here a New Mexico desert; an innocent Adam lies transfixed in a cave for six days; his Eve sinks her teeth into an apple. And if anyone is still skeptical about the film's mythic foundation, the biblical serpent is present in the form of the rattler the sheriff carries around in a cardboard box. The imagery is undeniably mythic and unrelievedly ugly: ominous mountains, blowing dust, a snake rattling against cardboard, a man pinned under adobe rubble and timber. However, it could have been worse; when the film was first previewed, it did not open with a shot of Paramount's snow-capped mountain; instead, a snake suddenly emerged from the sand. Obviously, Paramount dropped the opening and went back to its logo.

As it is, there are enough serpents in the film—of all varieties. The "Leo Minosa Special" transports the curiosity-seekers; copies of a country western ballad, "We're Coming, Leo," are hawked for a quarter. A carnival tent is pitched, and the desert becomes a fairground complete with ferris wheel and carousel. The Minosa Trading Post is thronged with customers; and admission to the Indian cliff dwellings, which once was free, keeps increasing along with the crowds.

But Leo cannot last the week. When Tatum realizes that Leo is dying, he orders the engineers to stop drilling and shore up the walls; Tatum's motives are a combination of selfishness and guilt. Wilder does not make it easy for his audience; Tatum is not a moral zombie like Diana Christensen (Faye Dunaway) in *Network*. In Wilder, even duplicitous hearts pump blood. Thus Tatum begins to feel slight pangs of guilt; his self-loathing, which until now had manifested itself in sarcasm, turns inward. He realizes, of course, that a dead man is no longer a news item; yet he is touched by Leo's ingenuousness. He is also appalled by Lorraine Minosa's indifference. When Leo senses he will not live to celebrate his wedding anniversary, he tells Tatum where he has concealed Lorraine's present, a furpiece. When Lorraine ridicules the gift ("They must have skinned a couple of hungry rats"), Tatum almost strangles her with it; in self-defense, she plunges a pair of scissors into his abdomen.

Leo expires on the sixth day as the grotesque creation myth comes to a close. Still, the serpentine imagery persists; Leo receives the last rites on a stick that passes across his face like a crawling snake. Tatum is also dying. Grabbing a microphone, he announces Leo's death to the crowd; the tent collapses, and the people disperse. Tatum returns to the newspaper office, boasting, "I'm a thousand-dollar-a-day newspaper man; you can have me for nothing." He falls forward, his face jutting into the frame.

Clearly, this is not the bluebird ending of *The Lost Weekend*; *The Big Carnival* is pure realism—life without frills. The ending rings true because Wilder pushes the plot to its logical conclusion where the trash queen kills the protagonist *à la Double Indemnity*; there is no Helen St. James around to regenerate Tatum, nor should there be. In fact, even in Don Birnam's case, Helen's regenerative powers seemed minimal.

Unfortunately, Wilder made *The Big Carnival*, which now has received the recognition it deserves, at the wrong time. In 1951, Americans were more interested in seeing Uncle Milty on the tube than in seeing themselves through Wilder's unflattering lens.

5

Barbwire Comedy:
A *Foreign Affair*, *Stalag 17*,
and *One*, *Two*, *Three*

FROM MAY to September 1945, Billy Wilder was Colonel Wilder, head of the film unit of the American Information Control Division in Germany, where he had been sent to assist in revitalizing the German film industry. Wilder's return to his homeland was hardly a sentimental journey; his mother and grandmother had died at Auschwitz, and the Berlin cemetery where his father was buried was so war-ravaged that Wilder had difficulty locating the gravesite. If a film were ever to grow out of the rubble of occupied Germany, it would never be a comedy; yet a comedy is exactly what Wilder made—a comedy that managed to offend Congress, the Department of Defense, and even its coauthor and producer, Charles Brackett, who found the subject unpatriotic—which is scarcely the right adjective for *A Foreign Affair*. "Ambivalent" is more accurate. In fact, *A Foreign Affair* is one of the most ambivalent movies Wilder ever made.

A Foreign Affair (1948)

The film opens with a plane flying over rows of gutted houses and concrete shells; from the air, Berlin looks like a porous relief map. A congressional committee is en route to Berlin to investigate reports that American GIs have forsaken USO clubs for cellar cafés where a smoky-voiced chanteuse leans against a steam pipe and sings her songs of disillusion. The committee will be in the city for five days, just enough time for a romance to develop between Iowa congresswoman Phoebe Frost (Jean Arthur) and Captain John Pringle (John Lund). However, Pringle's main concern is to keep the fact-finding committee from discovering the fact that his mistress is Erika von Schluetow (Marlene Dietrich), onetime

63

Marlene Dietrich as Erika and John Lund as Pringle in A Foreign Affair.

Credit: *Courtesy of Billy Wilder*

inamorata of a high-ranking Nazi. Neatly traced over the Phoebe-Pringle-Erika romantic triangle is another triangle—a political one whose sides are the Third Reich and the Berlin of the Occupation and whose base is the United States. Wilder has managed the superimposition so artfully that it is difficult to say if *A Foreign Affair* is a romantic comedy or a political one like Frank Capra's *State of the Union* (1948). However, Wilder's Berlin is not a city of heroes and villains like Capra's Washington, D.C. It would have been easy for Wilder to portray a Berlin of GIs dispensing Hershey bars to dirty-faced kids or repentant Nazis using Hitler's picture for a dart board; but when it came to Berlin, Wilder could not be simplisitic.

Hitler's Berlin was also Wilder's, and now it was a Berlin with an American sector. Wilder could not denounce the city where his film career began; besides, denunciation is not art. He also could not condone an ideology that sent his mother to a death camp. So, Wilder tries to be objective, which is not quite the same as being impartial. He allows Erika to explain that, for some, collaboration was the only means of survival. Wilder realizes that the swastika is an odious symbol of the Third Reich; yet, surely, one should be able to laugh at a German boy's obsession with drawing swastikas on everything, including the back of his father's coat. Certainly, the European Recovery Program was a noble endeavor; but even the committee cannot decide if the United States should offer economic aid without strings or find a way to keep Europe in its debt. As one congressman expresses it, "If you give a hungry man a loaf of bread, it's democracy; if you leave the wrapper on, it's imperialism."

A Foreign Affair cannot answer all the questions it raises, but Wilder's heart—and head—were in the right place. Again, he does not make it easy for the viewer because none of the three main characters is either admirable or despicable—and that includes the two Americans. Phoebe is a prude who braids her hair into a coronet that looks like a halo. Self-righteous and easily scandalized, she views her mission as a moral crusade to "fumigate" Berlin. Yet Wilder gives her a touching speech in which she describes her first love: a Southern Democrat whose politics she loathed. Later, she is transformed from a fumigator to a woman in love, speaking wistfully of herself as a swimmer on a gray sea rescued by the white boat of Captain Pringle. Pringle, on the other hand, seems to be the typical Wilder heel. He pulls Erika by the hair, calls her a blonde witch, and behaves more like a sadist than a rake. Yet he, too, is given his say; he was a lonely GI until, one day, a pair of open-toe shoes came along, and in them, the woman to end his loneliness. Even Erika gets an apologia: "Do you know what it was like to be a woman when the Russians came in?" she asks Phoebe. Once the mistress of a Nazi general, she now lives in a bombed-out hovel and speaks in terms of ruins rather than blocks.

There is a fourth voice balancing the other three; it belongs to Colonel Rufus Plummer (Millard Mitchell). In Plummer, the film's paradoxes are resolved. Although Plummer cannot sanction fraternization, he knows that wartime morality is unique; thus he looks the other way when he spots a silk stocking hanging out of Pringle's pants pocket. But Plummer also believes in expediency; thus he has no scruples about using Pringle as a decoy to trap Erika's Nazi lover. Plummer is a portrait of Wilder—crusty, tough, compassionate, and quintessentially American. "One family christened a boy DiMaggio Schultz. That's when I knew we won the war," he boasts.

Plummer resolves the paradoxes of *A Foreign Affair*; Erika resolves its moral ambivalence. As Erika, Marlene Dietrich was playing a familiar part—the lady with a past. However, the role of an apolitical German with Nazi connections was totally at odds with her World War II image of the glamour queen who traded her sequins for army fatigues and entertained GIs at the front lines. When Plummer orders Erika to a labor camp, she tries to charm him out of it, but to no avail. Yet Plummer permits her to stop at her apartment to change, sending two MPs to accompany her. Obviously, Erika will use her wiles on them; she lifts up her gown, noting that the soldiers can lift her over any puddles. Plummer immediately sends two more MPs to look after the first pair; then he sends an officer to keep tabs on them. Erika is incorrigible; even Plummer knows it. One doubts that she will ever see the inside of a labor camp.

Sending Erika to a labor camp would be the same as sending Marlene Dietrich to one. Dietrich possesses such a powerful mythology that it radiates through the character. Wilder was faithful to the Dietrich persona and to Erika by cleverly separating the trait from the character, the survival instinct from the survivor. Erika is the survivor, but it is Dietrich who embodies the will to survive. Thus one can admire the survival instinct without necessarily admiring the survivor.

A *Foreign Affair* as Realistic Film

In *A Foreign Affair* Wilder combined on-location filming with *mise-en-scène*. Complementing the authentic setting ("A large part of this film was photographed in Berlin," the credits state) are some unusually effective shots. Wilder never tires of exploring the myriad ways by which we perceive reality. We see others in a variety of ways, not merely face to face, but often against a background that frames the subject within an attractive geometric design—a rectangular doorway or window, a circular compact mirror, a rhomboid pane of glass.

When Pringle arrives at Erika's apartment, she is brushing her teeth in the bathroom; he sees her through a hole in the bathroom door. Ironically, the most realistic shots in the film are not of devastated buildings but of the Lorelei, the basement café where Erika performs. Whenever she sings, her image is reflected in panes of leaded glass. Wilder frequently uses the reflected image, which can be an embellishment as well as a means of perception or detection. Erika deliberately kisses Pringle without telling him that Phoebe is standing in the shadows; Pringle sees Phoebe silhouetted in the mirror. When Erika sings "Illusions," she works her way to the corner table where Phoebe and Pringle are sitting; a mirror reflects all three faces, as well as the violinist accompanying Erika. Reality is many things to Wilder: on-location shooting, long takes, verisimilitudinous subject matter, and a visual representation that surpasses the limits of sense experience without demeaning our source of perception. Wilder's camera not only sees more than the human eye; it sees creatively, also.

Stalag 17 (1953)

Just as Wilder found humor in the ruins of Berlin, he also found it in a German prisoner-of-war camp; or, more accurately, he found it in the Broadway play *Stalag 17*, by Donald Bevan and Edmund

Trzcinski, which opened in New York in 1951 and became a Billy Wilder film in 1953. *Stalag 17* was the first of four Broadway hits that Wilder adapted in the 1950s, the others being *Sabrina* (from *Sabrina Fair*), *The Seven Year Itch*, and *Witness for the Prosecution*.

Stalag 17 had all the makings of a flop. It premiered late in the 1950–51 season with virtually no advance sale to sustain it during the summer doldrums. Furthermore, there was not a single star in the all-male cast, yet the play had a successful run. Apparently, Broadway was ready for a salty comedy-melodrama about American GIs in a German POW camp in 1944. No doubt the novelty of the setting and the ribald humor contributed to its success. However, the play had one defect: the plot hinged on the presence of a spy the Germans planted in the barracks. Even a novice would know the spy was Price, the security officer. The same held true of the film, especially with blonde, Teutonic-looking Peter Graves in the part. But the spy's identity does not matter as much in the film as it did in the play because Wilder makes the unmasking of the informant an exercise in detection rather than a second-act revelation. In the play, an overheard conversation leads to the exposure of Price; in the film, the means are visual: a light cord and a chess piece—Wilder's invention, naturally.

Wilder was attracted to the play because of its odd mix of comedy and intrigue; but he was also fascinated by the character of Sefton (William Holden), who was a male Erika. Like Erika, Sefton is a born survivor. Erika survived World War II by selling her favors; Sefton survived a prison camp by selling everything— from silk stockings to white wine. His foot locker is a miniature PX. Sefton is the barracks profiteer, but Wilder makes him resourceful rather than loathsome. He runs a "mouse race" where the men can bet on their favorites; he brews schnapps from potato peelings and string; and he sets up an observatory for anyone wanting to see female prisoners lined up for delousing.

In the film, Sefton is not merely a con artist; he is a scrapper who learned to hustle at an early age and consequently developed a healthy contempt for the idle rich. He will trade his captors cigarettes for an egg which he fries in full view of his drooling buddies. In short, he is a typical Wilder heel. But heels intrigue

Stalag 17: "Animal" (Robert Strauss) and Sefton (William Holden) –bruised, bitter, but unbeaten.
Credit: Movie Star News

Wilder; they vacillate between self-love and self-loathing. Thus what seem to be contradictions in their character are merely manifestations of one side or the other of their personality.

Wilder's heels are usually capable of some action that is selfless, if not self-transcending. When the men beat up Sefton because they assume he is the spy, Sefton is understandably bitter but not vindictive. But now, he must unmask the spy; he can tolerate being called a racketeer, but not a stoolie. When he exposes Price, he reveals another facet of his character: a patriotism that is downright provincial. He mocks Price's surname, implying that originally it was "Preisling" or "Preishoffer."

Vindication is not enough; Sefton wants the fruits of heroism without the ballyhoo. Thus he volunteers to help a major escape to Switzerland. Before he leaves, Sefton bids a contemptuous farewell to the men of Stalag 17. He disappears into the tunnel beneath the barracks floor, but then he emerges for a moment with a grin and a salute. Who can hate a profiteer with Bill Holden's smile?

Barracks Art

Although a POW camp would hardly seem to be photographically interesting, *Stalag 17* contains some of Wilder's most impressive visuals. Two sequences are particularly memorable: Sefton's discovery of the spy's identity and the Christmas party when Sefton discloses it to the other men.

It is established early in the film that the spy and the German Corporal Schulz have a code: a loop in the light cord hanging from the ceiling means there is a message in the hollow black queen on the chessboard. Whoever receives the message unknots the cord, which then hangs freely. As far as the other prisoners are concerned, Sefton is the spy. As they parade around the barracks, singing "When Johnny Comes Marching Home," they ignore Sefton, who sits brooding in his bunk. Price, the security officer, is in the right of the frame. Spotting the loop in the cord, Price nonchalantly walks over to the chess table and removes the message from the queen. Quickly he unknots the cord. Sefton, who has been sitting in the darkness, suddenly sees the shadow of the swinging cord. The sequence ends with a chillingly dramatic touch: the cord dangling in the center of the frame and dominating it while the men march exuberantly in the background.

The climax is the Christmas party where Wilder brilliantly integrates contrasting moods and conflicting emotions without sacrificing any of the tension generated by a charged atmosphere. Despite the horseplay and the low humor, there is an understated poignancy about a party where bearded men dance together without eye contact, swaying dreamily and sexlessly as if closeness were all that mattered. Harry (Harvey Lembeck) has stuffed some straw under his hat to look like a blonde. For a moment, his buddy Stosh (Robert Strauss) thinks it is Betty Grable, his dream girl. To convey the illusion, Wilder uses a form dissolve; Harry in a pinup pose turns into Betty Grable. But when the shot fades, so does the mirage; and Stosh is heartbroken.

Sefton is still the pariah; thus he is excluded from the party. In an extraordinary shot, the camera starts tracking back from Price in the front of the frame and past the dancing men to Sefton at the back; then the camera retraces its route. It has traveled from the spy to his detector and back. Despite the manifold moods expressed in the sequence, one never has the impression of watching piecemeal activity. Sefton's bitterness has now cooled into detachment, and Price's self-confidence has turned into a cocky nonchalance. Both men are part of an emotionally complex atmosphere where illusions are shattered and hopes are sustained by listless dancing and the soft singing of "O Come, All Ye Faithful." The party needs some unity which Sefton provides when he unmasks Price.

Stalag 17 is now united. However, its unity has nothing to do with the yuletide spirit but rather with the desire for retribution. It has been an unusual Christmas party, for it will terminate in Price's death. In a scene reminiscent of Hitchcock's *Lifeboat* (1944) in which the survivors closed in on a Nazi and threw him overboard, the men hurl Price into the compound where he is killed by his fellow Germans. *Stalag 17* ends as it began—with the music of "When Johnny Comes Marching Home"; at the beginning, it sounded ominous; now it is whistled triumphantly.

One, Two, Three (1961)

Wilder made his second Berlin film thirteen years after *A Foreign Affair*, when the city's epithet changed from "occupied" to "divided." The summer of 1961 was an odd time to make a comedy about the Cold War. While Wilder was shooting *One, Two, Three*, a wall of cinder blocks, barbwire, and concrete was being erected to separate East and West Berlin. Politically, the situation became so tense that Wilder had to stop shooting in Berlin and move to Munich. Still, *One, Two, Three* gave Wilder another commercial success and again showed his ability to find laughter where others would find gloom.

Like *A Foreign Affair*, *One, Two, Three* attracted criticism from the humorless who felt it only aggravated the existing tension between the United States and the Soviet Union. At the 1963 Moscow Film Festival, screenwriter Abby Mann apologized to the Russians for films like *One, Two, Three* and promised them more movies like *The Grapes of Wrath* (1940). Abby Mann, one should remember, wrote the script for the serious—and ponderous—*Judgment at Nuremburg* (1961). Wilder was not interested in migrants or in collective guilt; he was determined to make a film that was so headline-fresh that the script was continually being altered to include topical references. He found the rudiments of a plot in Ferenc Molnár's one-act farce *President* (1926), also known as *Riviera* and originally entitled *One, Two, Three*.[1]

Molnár's play was a vehicle for the great comedian Max Pallenberg, who was famous for delivering his lines at a machine-gun clip. The plot involved a banker whose house guest, the daughter of a Swedish tycoon, marries a Socialist cab driver. The banker has about an hour to transform the cabbie into a suitable son-in-law—a feat he accomplishes by calling in an army of clothiers and tailors. The ruse succeeds, and the banker joins his wife for their vacation.

What would happen, Wilder wondered, if a similar situation developed in Cold War Berlin—with an American heiress marrying an East German Communist without her parents' knowlege? Make the heiress a scatterbrained Southern belle with the outrageous name of Scarlett Hazeltine; then her husband's name must be similarly outrageous—Otto Ludwig Piffl. What of Molnár's banker? Americans may be everywhere, but not in Berlin banks. But America's legacy—Coca-Cola—is everywhere; so Molnár's banker becomes an American Coke executive whose boss is none other than Scarlett's father. When the Hazeltines decide to come to Berlin, the executive has one day to turn Piffl into a capitalist with a lineage to boot. But what is a transformation without a twist? The deception is so successful that Piffl gets the London job the Coke executive wanted, while the latter is transferred to Atlanta.

One hurdle remained: Who could deliver dialogue with the triphammer speed of Max Pallenberg? Only one actor—James Cagney. Having played an O'Hara in *The Irish in Us* (1935), a Sullivan in *Angels with Dirty Faces* (1938), and a MacLean in *Captains of the Clouds* (1942), he would now add another Hibernian to his celluloid *vita*—Wilder's MacNamara.

Cagney by Wilder

Wilder seized the opportunity to exploit Cagney's screen persona. It is impossible to separate James Cagney from George M. Cohan, whom he portrayed so indelibly in *Yankee Doodle Dandy* (1942); likewise, one will always equate him with the gangster who pushed a grapefruit in Mae Clarke's face in *The*

Public Enemy (1931). Wilder quotes from both Cagney films. Exasperated by Piffl's tirades against the United States, Mac-Namara picks up a halved grapefruit and mutters: "How would you like a little fruit for dessert?" There is also a recurring sight gag in the form of an Uncle Sam cuckoo clock that plays "Yankee Doodle Dandy" on the hour. MacNamara is Sefton without the crewcut and cigar, speaking at breakneck speed; wheeling and dealing to boost Coca-Cola profits. If introducing Coke to the Soviet Union means getting a blonde for two bumbling comrades, MacNamara will supply one—even if it is a blonde in drag.

Thematically, *One, Two, Three* harks back to *Ninotchka*, where a militant Communist was also converted to capitalism; Piffl is really a male Ninotchka. Structurally, it was *A Foreign Affair* that guided Wilder in forging the screenplay. Both Berlin films began with geographical exposition. The opening montage of *One, Two, Three* with its contrast between the cosmopolitan West and the provincial East recalls the beginning of *A Foreign Affair*, where scenes of devastation alternated with tableaux of the Occupation (fraternizing GIs, a German woman proudly pushing a baby carriage decorated with American flags). Both films revolve around the effects of an unexpected arrival—the congressional committee in *A Foreign Affair*; the Hazeltines in *One, Two, Three*. Each ends with a chastened male reunited with his beloved—Pringle with Phoebe, MacNamara with his wife. In *A Foreign Affair*, the Russians were amiable vodka-swilling regulars at the Lorelei. There is no Lorelei in *One, Two, Three*; only the grand ballroom of the Hotel Potemkin, where an overage crooner sings "Yes, We Have No Bananas" in German. Wilder is suggesting that, since 1948, East Berlin has become the boondocks. In fact, Wilder kids everything about the Soviet Union—the 7:00 train that leaves promptly at 8:15; Communist clichés ("capitalist pig"; "we will bury you"); and a fondness for lurid similes (capitalism is compared to a dead herring in the moonlight).

However, unlike *A Foreign Affair, One, Two, Three* is not ambivalent. There is only one point of view: MacNamara's burly Americanism that is a conflation of jingoism and expediency. He is not especially appealing; but, then, no one else in the film is, either. This is the kind of comedy in which no one triumphs. Furthermore, Wilder was obsessed with pace; the film seems to have been cut to the tempo of the *Sabre Dance*, which is to *One, Two, Three* what the *William Tell* Overture is to "The Lone Ranger." What Wilder gained in speed, he lost in characterization. There is little warmth in the film, except for a touching moment during the reconciliation of the MacNamaras; yet Wilder even punctures that moment by using a gag at the fade out—a Pepsi coming out of the Coke machine. To its credit, *One, Two, Three* has some marvelously mordant satire, but it is clear that Wilder did not have the same feeling for the divided Berlin that he had for the occupied city. More important, the Cold War left a chill in himself and his script. Wilder's war was World War II. He understood occupied cities and prisoner-of-war camps; he did not understand East-West politics except in terms of farce.

6

September Songs: *Sabrina,*
The Seven Year Itch,
and *Love in the Afternoon*

IN THE 1950s Wilder made three May-December romances—
Sabrina, The Seven Year Itch, and *Love in the Afternoon.* There
were several reasons why Wilder infused them with an end-of-
summer mood. Casting was one of them. Linus Larrabee in
Sabrina was originally written for Cary Grant; when Humphrey
Bogart assumed the role, he was less than four years away from
death. Casting Cary Grant opposite Audrey Hepburn, as Stanley
Donen did a decade later in *Charade* (1963), would have resulted
in a sophisticated comedy; casting Humphrey Bogart opposite
Audrey Hepburn resulted in a romance between an older man and
a younger woman. Likewise, when Gary Cooper played opposite
Audrey Hepburn in *Love in the Afternoon,* he was in his mid
fifties—and looked it; Hepburn was in her late twenties and looked
eighteen. When Tom Ewell appeared on Broadway in *The Seven
Year Itch,* his costar was Vanessa Brown, a competent actress but
with no mythic allure. When Ewell recreated his role in the film, he
starred opposite Marilyn Monroe, who brought her own brand of
earthy divinity to the part; she played The Girl as a fertility goddess
who relied more on her fertility than on her godhead to liberate a
married man from the straitjacket of middle age.

Wilder started this cycle of films when he was in his late forties, a
fact that might account for his interest in the theme of the
rejuvenating female. His biographer, Maurice Zolotow, has argued that *Sabrina* and *Love in the Afternoon* reflect Wilder's
affection for his own daughter. Significantly, both films include a
father and daughter. *The Seven Year Itch* does not, but it had its
equivalent in the way Marilyn Monroe played certain scenes with
Tom Ewell; she would cuddle up to Ewell the way a teenager,

*Audrey Hepburn with a middle-aged Prince Charming, Gary
Cooper, in* Love in the Afternoon.
Credit: Movie Star News

awakening to her sexuality, might snuggle up to her father and give him a hug or a kiss tinged with playful eroticism.

Sabrina (1954)

Samuel Taylor's *Sabrina Fair* enjoyed a successful run on Broadway during the 1953–54 season and has become a summer-stock and little-theater favorite. The play was billed as a contemporary fairy tale, and indeed it was: a chauffeur's daughter, wooed by the millionaire sons of her father's employer, turns out to be an heiress because of her father's prudent investments. Ultimately, Wilder's adaptation became a study of a surrogate father-daughter relationship in which the heroine's devotion to her own father was partly responsible for her seeking a father substitute. However, Wilder was initially attracted to Taylor's play because it gave him the opportunity to return to one of his favorite characters: the commoner (Eve in *Midnight*, Sugarpuss in *Ball of Fire*, Susan in *The Major and the Minor*) who crosses over into the world of social registrants and stuffy intellectuals, ventilating their lives with a blast of healthy bourgeois air. Wilder retained the play's Cinderella theme, but dropped the last-minute revelation about the chauffeur's secret fortune. Too much prosperity can be cloying.

Yet Wilder wanted to keep something of the play's fairy-tale quality. *Sabrina Fair* opened with a once-upon-a-time prologue spoken on a darkened stage; Wilder used the same technique—a voice-over prologue in which Sabrina (Audrey Hepburn) describes life on the Larrabee estate in Long Island. *Sabrina Fair* begins with Sabrina's return to the estate after five years in Paris which transformed her from a gawky adolescent into a woman of the world. Wilder shows us Sabrina before the transformation. The first time one sees the fairy princess, she is literally up a tree; like a wood nymph, Sabrina is perched high on a branch, gazing longingly at the couples dancing on the terrace of the Larrabee mansion. Wilder's Sabrina is watching life from the outside, but it is a life in which she wants desperately to participate. If anyone should be waltzing to "Isn't It Romantic?" and "You Came Along," it is Sabrina, whose elfin face and ox-eyed purity would be a welcome distraction from the monotony of organdy gowns and orchid corsages. But Sabrina is the chauffeur's daughter, secretly in

Audrey Hepburn with another middle-aged Prince Charming, Humphrey Bogart, in *Sabrina*.

Credit: Margaret Herrick Library

love with playboy David Larrabee (William Holden); like Echo, she can only pine in silence.

Wilder has created a mood of heartbreaking delicacy in the opening sequence. Sabrina climbs down from the tree and watches David and his date through the window of an indoor tennis court. David knocks down the net, and he and the girl retire to the rear of the court. Weeping, Sabrina walks away. This is Sabrina's last night in Long Island; tomorrow, she is off to a Paris cooking school. The first sequence ends as poignantly as it began; a shot of Sabrina sitting in a rocking chair in her garret room dissolves to the tennis court where a feminine giggle answers the Lubitsch question, "Did they or didn't they?"

Despite the crystalline purity of the opening, *Sabrina* is not a perfect film. Sabrina's attempted suicide in the garage is a *hommage* to Hitchcock's *Shadow of a Doubt* (1943) where a psychopathic uncle planned a carbon-monoxide finale for his niece. Smoke rings emanating from exhaust pipes might have been

a good sight gag in a Jerry Lewis movie, but not in *Sabrina*.
Furthermore, Wilder's satiric gifts fail him in the cooking-school
sequence; a pancake-flat soufflé is not particularly funny. But once
Wilder returns to the theme of Cinderella and her fatherly prince
charming, he is on surer ground. Even at the cooking school,
Sabrina finds a paternal baron who repeats the advice her own
father gave her: "Don't reach for the moon." But a moon goddess
does not reach for her ancestral home; she returns to it, as Sabrina
does after two years in Paris.

Sabrina returns to Long Island as the transformed damsel in a
stunning Edith Head outfit. She is so sophisticated that David
Larrabee does not recognize her and tries to pick her up. The
"unrecognized woman" motif usually appears in tragedy or
melodrama—e.g., *Letter from an Unknown Woman* (1948),
Return from the Ashes (1965), *The Promise* (1978). But *Sabrina*
inverts the tragic convention without minimizing the effects of a
transformation that does not achieve its purpose. The transformed
Sabrina still experiences rejection but of a different sort; the
Larrabees want no part of her because Linus Larrabee (Humphrey
Bogart) has arranged for his brother to marry into a sugar dynasty.
To make sure his plan succeeds, Linus begins courting Sabrina but
soon falls in love with her. By altering the original play, Wilder was
able to make Linus one of his redemptive heels (Iscovescu in *Hold
Back the Dawn*, Pringle in *A Foreign Affair*, Flannagan in *Love in
the Afternoon*) who feigns love, only to fall headlong into it.

To resolve the plot, Wilder resorts to a *deus ex machina* which
one accepts only because the film has been operating on a fairy-
tale level. Sabrina is returning to Paris on the *Liberté*. As the ship
passes by the Larrabee building in lower Manhattan, Linus
discovers he has just enough time to hail a tugboat and head out to
the liner. Linus wins Sabrina, but she scores a double victory: a
husband and a father in the person—or persona—of Humphrey
Bogart.

The Seven Year Itch (1955)

After portraying life among the Long Island rich, Wilder headed
over to Manhattan's East Side, the setting of George Axelrod's
Broadway hit of the 1952–53 season, *The Seven Year Itch*.

Axelrod's comedy would challenge any filmmaker's ingenuity; the action was restricted to a single setting—a Gramercy Park apartment. Invariably, Wilder would have to open up the play; but he would not be able to free it from the confines of the proscenium as easily as he did *Sabrina Fair*, where the garden setting was not especially important to the plot. The setting of *The Seven Year Itch*, on the other hand, was indispensable to the plot, which involved a married man's shortlived summer dalliance with a girl subletting the apartment above his. Yet the lengthy apartment sequences in the film version work for two reasons: Wilder's ability to adapt to CinemaScope and his sensitive handling of the romance between Richard Sherman (Tom Ewell) and The Girl (Marilyn Monroe).

Some directors found it difficult adjusting to CinemaScope; George Stevens was fond of saying that the process was more suitable for photographing a python than a person because, in CinemaScope, the width of the projected image was 2.3 times its height; on the old familiar rectangle, the image was only 1.3 times as wide as it was high. Although CinemaScope hardly seemed the right process for making a comedy with several fantasy sequences, Wilder made it work. He repeated on widescreen what he had done earlier in *The Lost Weekend* flashbacks; for Sherman's fantasies in *The Seven Year Itch*, he used a combination pandissolve, with reality slipping gently into fantasy as the camera imitates the rhythm of withdrawal by slow panning.

In the first fantasy, Sherman envisions his prim secretary as a nymphomaniac. He is left of frame; as the fantasy materializes on the right, the camera balances the movement from the real to the imaginary by panning left to right. One fantasy is especially complex because it transmogrifies events that had occurred earlier. Previously, The Girl, who does television commercials, told Sherman about the time she got her toe caught in the bathtub faucet and had to call a plumber. Sherman now imagines what might happen if The Girl divulged their affair on television. Wilder pans away from Sherman on the right, dissolving to The Girl in the tub as she tells the fussy plumber (Victor Moore in a cameo part) about her lecherous neighbor. Then the camera pans left to right, past Sherman and over to the plumber, who is repeating the story to a group of shocked listeners. A dissolve to Sherman is followed by an unusual tracking shot. The camera tracks up to The Girl in the television studio as she is about to go on the air; the forward tracking stops when The Girl's face is the size of a television close-up. Then the camera tracks back, revealing her face on an actual television set. But is not just any set; it is the set on the porch of the Maine lodge where Sherman's son is listening to The Girl denounce his father as a sex fiend. The boy calls to his mother, and the sequence ends with a dissolve to Sherman who looks ashen, as if he had witnessed everything.

Wilder's creative filming of the fantasy sequences proves he was not remaking *The Secret Life of Walter Mitty*; his sympathetic portrayal of the romance between Sherman and The Girl makes it plain that he was not making a bedroom farce. Wilder treated Marilyn Monroe respectfully, never using her body as if it were a *Playboy* centerfold. Since Sherman's point of view dominates the film, one will occasionally see her as a sex object; hence the shot of Marilyn's banjolike behind. But Wilder minimizes such shots; in fact, he rarely shoots Marilyn in close-up. In the film's most famous shot, where a blast of air from the subway grating sends her dress fluttering above her knees, the camera behaves like a gentleman.

The fact that The Girl is more compassionate in the film than she was in the play is due to Marilyn's performance and Wilder's changes in the original characterization. In the film, the character is literally a golden girl, radiating warmth from her first appearance. When we first see The Girl, she is standing behind the glass door of the apartment house, waiting to be buzzed in; backlit by the sun, she is a shimmer of gold.

However, The Girl is not simply a goddess-on-earth; her divinity resides in the body of a woman. She is a Wilder rarity: a woman who understands men. In a speech that does not appear in Axelrod's play, she expresses her contempt for the masculine, sexually confident male she constantly encounters at parties; the type to whom she is really attracted is the shy, gentle loner. The Girl has given Sherman confidence in his own low-keyed masculinity. "If I were your wife," she says, "I'd be jealous of you." Before Sherman goes off to Maine to join his wife and son, The Girl gives him a message for Mrs. Sherman—a kiss.

Although Wilder had problems directing Marilyn, who was never on time and continually forgetting her lines, he found an

Tom Ewell and Marilyn Monroe in a production still from *The Seven Year Itch*. (In the film, this is a simple thighs-to-feet shot, discreetly photographed.)

engaging comedienne beneath the open-mouth pose. In certain scenes, Marilyn actually parodied the very image Hollywood expected her to promote. When she shows Sherman how she does a commercial for a toothpaste that keeps breath "kissing sweet," her face becomes erotically feline; the eyes close partly, and the lips purr. Clearly, this is Marilyn imitating one of her imitators. There is also a natural, uninhibited quality about her performance. When she describes a photo of herself in *U.S. Camera* as "one of those artistic pictures," she innocently tugs at the neckline of her pink blouse.

In Axelrod's play, there was no question that Sherman and The Girl committed adultery; Wilder prefers to suggest rather than state. Did they or didn't they? The script says they didn't, but the visuals equivocate. There is an air of seduction accomplished and enjoyed, a parting kiss between lovers. When Sherman says he is sorry he cannot stay for breakfast, The Girl's reply, "Don't ever be sorry," is obviously code. Sorry for what? Missing breakfast or being unfaithful? When The Girl discovers that prying up a few floorboards can bring her down to him on the unused staircase connecting their apartments, the camera tracks up to her as she descends. At first, one thinks it is another fantasy; but it is really The Girl with a hammer in one hand and a toothbrush in the other. Fade out on The Girl and in on Sherman asleep on the sofa. But what happened between the fades? Presumably, Sherman discovered a way of bridging the gap between December and May.

Love in the Afternoon (1957)

The Seven Year Itch opened like a madcap farce with patchwork credits, squares flapping open, and Wilder's name springing out of the frame like a jack-in-the-box; then, the film went on to become a comedy with moments of genuine tenderness. *Love in the Afternoon* opens with a wink; the credits start as a woman discreetly pulls down a shade. Then comes an "Everybody Does It" prologue—a montage of sight gags punctuated by Maurice Chevalier's rakish commentary as he shows us lovers embracing on the left bank; on the right bank; existentialists kissing despairingly in a café; and even poodles nose to nose. "There is married love and illicit love; this is where I come in," the voice says. And this is where the prologue ends and the film begins; where Chevalier's voice joins the character he is playing—Claude Chevasse, a private detective specializing in adultery.

Love in the Afternoon followed *Sabrina* by three years; it was Wilder's second and last film with Audrey Hepburn as well as his second and last portrayal of the father-daughter relationship. In *Sabrina*, Wilder did not explore the bond between Sabrina and her father because, in the film, Thomas Fairchild was not a major role. In *Love in the Afternoon*, Chevasse is not a secondary part; thus Wilder can portray his relationship with his daughter Ariane (Audrey Hepburn) in greater detail.

Early in the film, Wilder uses a long shot to depict the kind of life the widower and his daughter have together. As Chevasse enters their flat, Ariane is practicing the cello; Wilder frames both of them in the same shot. There is no fluttery rush to the door, no outstretched arms, no squealed greetings. Father and daughter know each other's habits. This is a typical day in the Chevasse household.

And Ariane is a typical innocent yearning for her first encounter with experience. When she overhears a jealous husband planning to kill his wife's lover, she goes to the man's hotel to warn him. A sense of duty is only part of her motive; she also wants to enter an adult world she knows only in euphemisms. Her father deals with cheating wives, whores, and adulterers. To Ariane, such people do not exist; there are only coquettes, courtesans, and roués. Even when Ariane begins her afternoon trysts with Flannagan (Gary Cooper), the American she saved from the jealous husband, that is all they are—trysts, dalliances, love (as opposed to lovemaking) in the afternoon.

Metaphor is all, and all is metaphor. The first time Ariane agrees to spend the afternoon with Flannagan, she simply removes her gloves and hands them to him. Later, when she arrives at his suite, draped in ermine, he asks her to remove the fur. The coat falls to the floor. Close-up of ermine. Fade out. Wilder takes an elliptical approach to their romance because Flannagan and Ariane so resemble father and daughter that, to go beyond the removal of gloves or the dropping of a coat, would be incestuous.

Even if Wilder wanted to be perverse and discard metaphor, he could not alter the mythological subtext that Gary Cooper and Audrey Hepburn created by their presence in the film. Both stars had screen personae ideally suited to the characters. Hepburn always exuded a cautious sensuousness, like a rosebud eager to open but afraid of losing its petals. Cooper was always the loner, the reticent lover, the cowpoke who mocked his own lack of sophistication by affecting a monosyllabic vocabulary and the air of a yokel. If Flannagan is the swinger the script claims he is, then he swings with a drawl, and his orgies are as shocking as a hoedown.

Ariane and Flannagan are, to use the movie cliché, made for each other. She needs a father whom she can charm with her blooming womanhood; he needs a daughter who is fascinated by older men. Ariane not only brings purity to their romance; she also offers Flannagan a type of woman he has never known—a moon goddess whose virginity is never really lost because it is always restored. Thus what might have been a repugnant relationship if an aging playboy like Errol Flynn were Flannagan or a love-child type like Sue Lyon were Ariane, becomes an afternoon liaison between a princess and her middle-aged prince, with all the glamour and lack of unsavoriness that "liaison" implies.

Wilder is not merely decking out a May-December romance with a metaphorical trim. Metaphor serves the plot, and Wilder has always been conscious of careful plotting. Therefore, he constructs the second half of the film in such a way that it duplicates the first, which began with a jealous husband's visit to Chevasse's flat. At a Turkish bath, the husband turns up in the same steam room with Flannagan, who is eager to learn the identity of his lady of the afternoon. The husband refers Flannagan to Detective Chevasse.

To establish a visual connection between the two visits to Chevasse's flat, the jealous husband's and Flannagan's, Wilder uses the same type of composition: a long shot that includes father, daughter, and client. In the first part of the film, Chevasse and his client were in the office, as Ariane looked out at them from her room. Similarly, when Flannagan arrives at the flat, Wilder creates a triptych effect in one shot: Flannagan standing in the entrance way, Ariane washing her hair in the bathroom, and Chevasse closing the folding doors so he and his client will not be disturbed. Such compositions automatically convey an atmosphere of realism; for reality is beginning to loom over the horizon of operetta as a father must confront his daughter with the shoddy way he makes a living; and a daughter must admit to her father how she spends her afternoons. But Chevasse is not a puritan, and Ariane is not a whore. In a moment of great poignancy, Chevasse realizes how important illusion is for Ariane. "She's such a little fish. Throw her back in the water," he begs Flannagan after he informs him that Ariane is his daughter.

Wilder adapted *Love in the Afternoon* from Claude Anet's novel *Ariane* (1920).[1] He retained only the germ of Anet's plot—a young girl who could not bear to tell her lover that she was a virgin when they met—and the ending. At seventeen, Anet's Ariane Nicolaevna delights in her power to bewitch men. In love with her youth and her femininity, she yearns to play the entire female repertoire—*femme fatale*, temptress, adventuress; but not yet wife. She torments her history teacher with her coyness; she taunts her suitor, who is twice her age, with stories about her lovers. But the truth is that Ariane has no lovers. When she goes off to Moscow to study at the university, she meets Constantin Michael, a world traveler who can quote Heine and Vigny. Since Constantin expects his mistresses to be experienced, Ariane leads him to believe she has had many lovers.

Finally, she knows she must tell him the truth. On the eve of Constantin's departure for St. Petersburg, Ariane tells him she has a secret that she will reveal at the train station. Then she decides to divulge the truth in the darkness of their room: he was her first lover. Constantin, however, says nothing although he remembers the drops of blood on the sheet after their first night together. The next day, at the train station, both of them are silent. As the train begins to pull out, one thinks it will take Constantin out of Ariane's life forever when, suddenly, he sweeps her up into his arms and takes her aboard. *"Tais-toi! tais-toi!"* (Be quiet! Be quiet!) he implores, kissing away her tears.

Paul Czinner's film version, *Ariane* (1931), ended the same way but without any words being spoken. Wilder adds one word to Anet's "Be quiet!" At the end of *Love in the Afternoon*, Ariane is seeing Flannagan off; she is still trying to convince him she is a woman of the world. He, of course, now knows otherwise. As the train begins to move, Ariane rushes along the platform, reminding Flannagan of all the men she will be able to see in his absence. As the train picks up speed, Flannagan lifts her aboard and carries her to a seat in the back. "Be quiet, Ariane," he says. Note that Flannagan simply does not say, "Be quiet" like Anet's Constantin. He has spoken her name for the first time, acknowledging her in the most basic way.

But, as is usually the case with Wilder, the tears dry quickly, and a twinkle lights the eye. Chevasse now becomes the voice of Maurice Chevalier returning to speak the epilogue; Flannagan and Ariane are now "serving a life sentence" in New York. Even their marriage is expressed in the language of euphemism. But how else can one describe a union between Audrey Hepburn and Gary Cooper?

7

The Human Comedies: *Some Like It Hot, The Apartment,* and *Avanti!*

Some Like It Hot (1959)

IT WOULD NOT be hyperbole to call *Some Like It Hot* a comic masterpiece. It has the classic comic plot of disguise, deception, and intrigue where a single complication generates a series of subplots the way a single pebble creates concentric ripples in a pool. *Some Like It Hot* also possesses a quality found in the best comedies—a sense of humanity and an attitude of compassion for the lunatics and lovers who play the fool for our sake. Humanity is the last feature one would associate with a film about two musicians who witness a Chicago gangland slaying, disguise themselves as women, and join an all-girl band en route to Palm Beach. It may sound even more paradoxical to assert that Wilder achieves this sense of humanity through parody; yet he does. Wilder reduces his characters to their parodistic core—to their cartoon selves. A typical satirist would stop there—with a caricature; but Wilder puts flesh on their skeletal frames—human flesh. Now the characters are laughable—not as caricatures or stereotypes, but as clowns. One laughs at stereotypes because they are exaggerations of the real; it is safe to laugh at them because they are dehumanized, and we are not; they are mechanical, but we have free will. One does not laugh at a clown; one laughs at his antics. A clown is not a distortion of reality but an externalization of reality in all its bizarre shades, from whiteface to motley.

It is easier to think of *Some Like It Hot* as parody if one recalls William Golding's belief that parody is "subtly rooted in admiration."[1] The novelist meant that one can admire a work and at the same time enjoy the incongruity that results when the work is transferred from its original context to one where it will provoke an

87

entirely different reaction—laughter instead of tears, mirth instead of sobriety. True parodists understand ambivalence; thus they can gently kid the very thing they admire.

For *Some Like It Hot* Wilder chose the classic way of achieving unity: selectivity. He selected one comic device, parody, and made it the source of all the others. The film opens parodistically. A hearse comes down a snow-covered street. Gunfire erupts, and bullets perforate the coffin that begins to leak; the liquid is liquor. Although the setting is Al Capone's Chicago, the opening shot recalls that familiar stretch of pavement on the Warner Brothers lot known as the "New York Street" featured in countless gangster films of the 1930s and 1940s; it was always dimly lit and slick from rain, and a coupe was always careening around the corner. Wilder is quoting from those Warner Brothers movies of the 1930s with their bootleggers and their bootleggers' wars. In fact, the opening scene is a montage of *The Public Enemy* (1931), *Angels with Dirty Faces* (1938), and *The Roaring Twenties* (1939); and the casting of George Raft as the Capone figure, "Spats" Colombo, enhances the Warner Brothers mood.

In addition to parodying the Warner Brothers atmosphere he so brilliantly evokes, Wilder also has fun with a familiar movie type: the witness to a crime. These characters can either take it on the lam, like Abbott and Costello in *Hit the Ice* (1943); discover that nobody believes them, like Barbara Stanwyck in *Witness to Murder* (1954); or change their identity and profession, like Deanna Durbin in *Lady on a Train* (1945). To Wilder, the comic potential would be doubled if the characters, Joe (Tony Curtis) and Jerry (Jack Lemmon), kept their profession but changed their sex.[2]

Drag has always been a perennial source of humor. In movies, one thinks of Bob Hope in a coconut shell bra in *Road to Zanzibar* (1941) and Cary Grant straightening his seams in *I Was a Male War Bride* (1949). But the typical Hollywood movie never attempted to feminize the men. We laugh precisely because the transformation is incomplete; there is always a hairy leg beneath the gown, a trace of five-o'clock shadow, or just a sense of physical discomfort at being girdled and gartered. However, Wilder accomplishes a perfect transformation; when Joe and Jerry become Josephine and Geraldine, they have become so feminized that they fool the eternal feminine herself—Marilyn Monroe as Sugar Kane, who strums a ukelele and sings in the all-girl band.

The transformation is more than just falsies and skin without stubble. Sugar is immediately attracted to the disguised pair, and they to her—but for different reasons. Sugar wants friendship, and the men want Sugar. Ironically, what Sugar thinks is friendship turns out to be love; and what the men originally thought were feminine traits become natural to them. Jerry decides he prefers the name Daphne to Geraldine; he also becomes obsessed with marrying a millionaire. Joe tells Jerry to fix his face. Wilder is kidding one of America's most cherished articles of faith—an unwavering belief in the two-sex system. Wilder is not slashing at our sexual parochialism as if he were wielding the scythe of Cronos. He is cynical about sexual stereotypes but he is also compassionate toward those who find themselves sexually type-cast—in particular, Joe, Jerry, and Sugar. Wilder will break the spell of stereotypy and transform the three of them into human beings.

Initially, Joe and Jerry were cardboard figures: the duke and the jester, the stud and the zany. We have seen them in every college film and in every college: the star athlete and his impressionable roommate; the big man on campus and the bespectacled book-worm who idolizes and envies him. Yet Joe and Jerry need each other the way the straight man needs the comic, and vice versa. However, once Sugar enters their lives, she disrupts their friend-ship. Sugar is Leslie Fiedler's malefic anima who threatens male camaraderie. Joe and Jerry are now rivals for Sugar's affections; but in their present disguise, they find courting a woman some-what difficult. Joe, the cleverer of the two, fakes a Cary Grant accent and impresses Sugar with his mythical wealth; but Jerry cannot regain his manhood so easily. He grows petulant and tries to sabotage his friend's romance.

Ironically, while Joe is romancing Sugar in the guise of a millionaire yachtsman, Jerry/Daphne is being courted by a real millionaire—Osgood Fielding (Joe E. Brown). And just as Sugar is succumbing to Joe's charms, Jerry/Daphne is succumbing to Osgood's. Jerry enjoys the attention; but does he enjoy it as Jerry or as Daphne? Jerry would like Sugar to rock him in a cradle of love; but Daphne talks openly of an unconsummated marriage with

Osgood that would end in annulment and alimony. In a Pirandellian way, the trick has become the reality. Every hidden trait that Jerry had, even those that most of us would regard as feminine, comes out in the masquerade. Yet it is a masquerade that never really ends; for once Jerry drops the mask, Osgood dons it. Jerry must tell Osgood he cannot marry him. First, he tries enumerating his inadequacies as a wife, but to no avail. Finally, he yanks off his wig and says, "Damn it, I'm a man." "Well, nobody's perfect," Osgood replies in a line that is certainly the kiss off to sexual stereotypy.

To humanize Sugar, Wilder stripped away the gold digger's facade Howard Hawks had Marilyn assume in *Gentlemen Prefer Blondes* (1953); he replaced the carnal queen with the vulnerable sex goddess with the Bambi eyes. Marilyn was now little girl lost; for once, her eyes did not ring up potential sales like a cash register. By finding the child within Marilyn's overpublicized body, Wilder enabled her to give her best screen performance as Sugar.

Sugar is a loner who carries a flask in her stocking and has little in common with the other members of the band. Jokes about one-legged jockeys do not interest her. Thus she finds in Josephine and Geraldine the sisters of her dreams. She can climb onto an upper berth and cuddle up with Geraldine the way one child seeks out another for warmth. Men have abused Sugar, but she is not bitter about it. Always the child, even in her metaphors, she complains about getting "the fuzzy end of the lollipop." One waits desperately for Joe to reveal himself and put an end to Sugar's unhappiness. He does, but not in the way one expects.

Sugar is on the bandstand doing a solo, "I'm Through With Love." It is a genuinely touching moment, for the singer has become the song. Suddenly, Joe, still in drag, jumps up and kisses her on the mouth. "Josephine!" Sugar cries. She is surprised but not shocked; the princess is never shocked by disenchantment.

No discussion of *Some Like It Hot* would be complete without mentioning Wilder's handling of the sequence in which Joe is romancing Sugar on board a yacht while Osgood is wooing Jerry Daphne in a roadhouse. Wilder could have crosscut the scenes, but the effect of a double seduction occurring simultaneously—one succeeding, the other too ludicrous even to fail—would have been lost. Instead, Wilder used a swish pan, where the camera would swing from one place to the other—from the yacht to the roadhouse—creating a momentary blur. Since Joe is feigning impotence to win Sugar, a swish pan would literally throw the viewer off the yacht when the situation grew too intimate.

Wilder would swish pan on a punch line; the effect was similar to a blackout in a musical revue when a skit would end with a punch line, and the stage would go dark. When Joe explains to Sugar that his sex life is comparable to smoking without inhaling, Sugar says, "So inhale!" Swish pan to Osgood and Jerry/Daphne dancing a tango; Osgood complains that his partner is leading. Swish pan back to the yacht; and before one knows it, Joe is inhaling.

"Some like it hot, but I prefer classical music," Joe informs Sugar when he is masquerading as the yachtsman. For those who like it hot, for those who like it classical, Wilder has made the perfect comedy. He asks us to make one change in Puck's famous line in *A Midsummer Night's Dream* (III, 2): "Lord, what fools these mortals be!" Wilder would have us say "lovable fools."

The Apartment (1960)

Bud Baxter (Jack Lemmon) and Fran Kubelik (Shirley Mac-Laine) are the lovable fools of *The Apartment*. However, the film did not inspire love in the hearts of some of our leading critics. To Stanley Kauffmann, it had a "tasteless gimmick"; Hollis Alpert termed it a "dirty fairy tale"; Dwight Macdonald found it "immoral," "dishonest," and "without style or taste." The gimmick—an accountant in an insurance firm who makes his apartment available to his superiors for their little adulteries—may be tasteless, but Wilder's treatment is not. Wilder made some dirty fairy tales that will be discussed in the next chapter; *The Apartment* is not one of them. Let us say that *The Apartment* is like a valentine where the lace edging is a bit frayed, but the red heart in the center is still bright and satin-soft. Bud and Fran are both innocents, babes in the dirty woods of big business. Bud divorces his key-lending from a moral context; it is something one does to advance, rather like flattering the boss or running errands for the higher-ups. Fran is a waif in need of a protector; she lives with her sister and brother-in-law and has virtually no life of her own. That Fran would have an affair with a married man is understandable;

that she would attempt suicide when he cannot marry her is
plausible; that she attempts it in Bud's apartment is not surprising,
since her lover is the personnel director who has acquired the
exclusive right to Bud's duplicate key; and that she would find her
ideal in Bud is inevitable.

Bud is the least odious of Wilder's schemers, and it is because of
Jack Lemmon's performance that audiences find him endearing.
Lemmon is the Con Man Kid; his eyes are not beads but buttons
that seem to have popped off a child's play suit. Wilder's
sympathies are clearly with him. Bud's efforts to advance only
intensify his loneliness. He stands behind the stoop watching a
colleague and a blonde race up the steps to his apartment while he
must retire to a bench on Central Park South until they have
finished. In an extreme long shot running the length of the screen,
Bud sits by himself, bundled in a raincoat; the wind drives the
leaves along a row of benches that seems to stretch out to infinity.
The camera tracks in, stopping short of a close-up and fading out
instead.

In *Some Like It Hot*, Wilder achieved humanity through parody;
in *The Apartment*, he achieves it through a moral balance. There
are no villains in *The Apartment*. The closest one comes to a villain
is the personnel director, Sheldrake (Fred MacMurray), a name
that must have personal significance for Wilder since there is a
Sheldrake in *Sunset Boulevard*, *The Big Carnival*, and *Kiss Me,
Stupid*. Obviously, one is supposed to think of the duck with black
and white plumage; but that is what Sheldrake is—black and white
mingled into a dirty gray. Sheldrake is not a blackguard; he
simply has the look of unlaundered linen. Here, again, is another
instance of perfect casting. Fred MacMurray was never villain-
ous—smarmy but not evil. Even in *Double Indemnity*, he was a
slippery charmer who ran out of lubricant when he met Phyllis
Dietrichson. In *The Apartment*, he is the familiar suburban
adulterer: the respectable husband and father who is never on time
for dinner because he is with his secretary, or, when he tires of her,
with the elevator operator. Inevitably, Sheldrake will pay for his
adultery; if anything, *The Apartment* is a moral fairy tale because
Sheldrake pays doubly. Sheldrake and his kind live by back-
scratching. But when the itch is not relieved, the flesh is clawed;
and when a favor is not returned, the ingrate is flayed. Thus Shel-

drake's ex-secretary, also his ex-mistress, informs Mrs. Sheldrake of her husband's infidelity with Fran. However, now that he is available, Fran is not.

There is adultery and there is art; the former is Wilder's subject matter, the latter his forte. Perhaps more than any other film, *The Apartment* shows Wilder's gift for realism both in *mise-en-scène* and character portrayal. The building where Bud lives is one of those brownstones off Central Park West where the sidewalks are lined with garbage cans and where, in late autumn, the street lamps make the pavement glisten after a downpour. Everything about the area, including the actual walk-up apartment, exudes a cozy seediness and a loneliness that is bearable because it has not degenerated into desperation. Physically, Bud's apartment has a lived-in look that is rare in Hollywood movies. A wall divides the narrow bedroom from the walk-in kitchen; at times, Wilder will include both rooms in the same shot. Wilder treats the apartment as if it were a character, giving it the same tasteful sloppiness that characterizes its tenant, who can strain spaghetti with a tennis racket and at the same time decorate his living room walls with Picasso prints. But the apartment is also central to the plot, and Wilder assigns each room a specific function in its unfolding—a suicide attempt in the bathroom, an abortive New Year's dinner in the living room, and a vigil in the bedroom, where Bud keeps watch over the sleeping Fran.

As one might expect, objects are also indispensable to the plot. The key object is, of course, Bud's key. It is odd that the moralists failed to see the rich ambivalence Wilder attached to the key. Bud's duplicate key won him Sheldrake's favor and the dream key—the key to the executive washroom. However, when Sheldrake requests the apartment key for a New Year's Eve fling with Fran, Bud reciprocates by giving him a key—the key to the executive washroom. Finally, Bud has made a regenerative decision; he has rejected the pimp's cynosure.

The Apartment would not be a Wilder film without a mirror. Discovery or recognition by means of a mirror is only dramatically effective if the mirror is part of the setting or is one of the character's accessories. Sometimes, recognition through the looking glass is merely ludicrous. In horror films, for example, the lycanthrope watches his transformation in a mirror. Given the agony he is experiencing, there is little reason for his being so narcissistic. When Bud discovers a broken compact in his apartment, he returns it to Sheldrake, who laughingly tells him that a girl threw it at him the previous night. At this point, Bud does not know that the girl was Fran. Later, Bud, the rising executive, buys a bowler and asks Fran's opinion of it. She hands him her compact, and he sees his reflection in the cracked glass. The flash of recognition is emotionally devastating, for both Bud and the audience.

During their last rendezvous in the apartment, Sheldrake tells Fran he cannot marry her. When he leaves, she goes into the bathroom, not knowing she is in Bud's apartment. She sees a bottle of sleeping pills reflected in the shaving mirror. Wilder had used the same technique before—the shaving mirror that revealed the pistol in the bathroom sink in *The Lost Weekend*; the compact mirror that revealed the presence of "Spats" Colombo and his henchmen in the hotel lobby in *Some Like It Hot*. In every case, the mirror was a vital prop as natural to the action as to the character using it, and the characters in *The Apartment* are among the most natural Wilder has ever created.

At the end of *The Apartment*, Bud and Fran are sitting on a couch, playing gin rummy. "I absolutely adore you," Bud rhapsodizes. "Shut up and deal," Fran replies, checking his effusiveness with mock flippancy. Like "Nobody's perfect," "Shut up and deal" is the kind of one-liner that cannot be topped; just as *The Apartment* is the kind of film that cannot lead to a sequel or a remake. Naturally, one wonders if the couple will remain as incorruptible as they were at the fade out. Wilder may have wondered also, but he wisely refrained from continuing their story. He has never given us quite the same pair of lovers again (Earl and Molly of *The Front Page* come close); but in *Avanti!* he ponders what might have happened if the same types met when the Bud figure is middle aged and married; and the Fran is spunky and single.

Avanti! (1972)

Avanti! was the second Samuel Taylor play that Wilder adapted. Unlike the successful *Sabrina Fair*, however, Taylor's *Avanti!* was

Two with Jack Lemmon: (top) with Shirley MacLaine as the eternal innocents in *The Apartment*; (bottom) with Juliet Mills as innocents at the crossroads in *Avanti!*

one of the failures of the 1967–68 Broadway season. A revised
version entitled *A Touch of Spring* fared somewhat better in
London in 1975. Wilder approached *Avanti!* the same way he
approached *Sabrina Fair*; he kept the armature of the plot but
provided his own dynamo. In addition to freeing the action from
its boxlike setting—a hotel room in Rome—and relocating the
characters on the island of Ischia, Wilder even went so far as to
change the names of the leads; Taylor's Sandy and Alison became
Wendell Armbruster (Jack Lemmon) and Pamela Piggott (Juliet
Mills).

What appealed to Wilder about *Avanti!* was its premise that was
as macabre as it was poignant. When an American businessman
arrives in Italy to reclaim his father's body, he discovers that his
father died in an automobile accident along with a female
companion whose daughter is also in Italy, arranging for her
mother's body to be shipped back to England. Sandy and Alison,
as they are called in the play, learn that Alison's mother was more
than the traveling companion of Sandy's father; she was his
mistress. Sandy's father flew to Italy every May to spend a month
with her. Naturally, Sandy and Alison fall in love; and rather than
let Sandy's marriage stand between them, they decide to adopt the
arrangement their parents had and spend one adulterous month
together in Italy each year.

Wilder must have been thinking of *The Apartment* when he was
working on *Avanti!* since he repeats many of the same motifs: the
guileless pair (Bud and Fran/Armbruster and Pamela); the preda-
tors (Sheldrake/Bruno, the blackmailing valet); the Good Samari-
tans (the Dreyfusses/Carlucci, the hotel manager); blackmail (the
key for advancement/incriminating pictures for money). However, because of age and outlook, the decisions the couples make
are quite different. Bud and Fran were young enough to buck the
system. Armbruster is not a rising executive; he is middle aged and
successful. Pamela, although younger, is mature enough to know
that life involves compromises that are rarely fifty-fifty but more
like eighty-twenty, in favor of society. Thus they give society
eleven months of the year in return for one unconventional month
of their own.

In adapting the play, Wilder kept only Taylor's introduction (the
event that brought the couple to Italy) and the resolution (the

adoption of their parents' yearly ritual). He deleted Taylor's entire supporting cast that included the wife, an embassy attaché, a bisexual Italian, and a flamboyant filmmaker who was the essence of Gucci. Wilder had to make these changes. Samuel Taylor's forte was comedy of manners, but too much about the play was mannered. Wilder wanted to make a film about innocence and experience that would also touch the heart. He succeeded because he shaped the script around the moral contours of *The Apartment*, where there were no real villains but just nasties who got what they deserved.

Wilder, who was not above showing a bit of behind in the liberated 1970s, staged a moonlight swim in the nude for Armbruster and Pamela which became grist for a blackmailer's camera. The swim was not merely an opportunity to photograph the leads from their singularly unattractive backsides; it was also the impetus for the denouement. In the play, the couple decided to bury their parents in Rome, although how they planned to circumvent the bureaucracy was never explained. Wilder has the blackmailer killed by a jealous mistress; the blackmailer's body is shipped back to the United States as Mr. Armbruster, so the real Mr. Armbruster can be buried in Ischia. The switch-of-bodies motif derives from "The Widow of Ephesus" in Petronius's *Satyricon*, where the widow allows her lover to substitute her husband's corpse for the stolen body of a crucified slave. It may have been a grisly touch, but it provided the motivation.

Despite the twists and complications that Wilder added to Taylor's play, he did not disturb the love story at the center; in fact, he turned drawing-room adultery into a realistic affair by his adroit casting. Juliet Mills, looking fetchingly plump, was the proper foil for the angular Jack Lemmon, whose nervous system seemed to run on caffeine. Yet Wilder never trivializes the tragedy that brought them together. When they enter the morgue to identify their parents, Wilder captures its stillness with a long shot that he holds until a shaft of sunlight comes through the circular window. Pamela leaves daffodils on each corpse, a gesture that anticipates Michael York's placing a single rose on Fedora's breast at the end of *Fedora* (1978).

To portray the growing love between Armbruster and Pamela, Wilder uses one of his favorite devices—transformation—but as a means of humanizing the characters, not of disguising them. Armbruster starts wearing his father's coat; Pamela, her mother's dress. Then they start using the same nicknames their parents had for each other—Willie and Kate. Interestingly, *Avanti!* is Wilder's only film in which an act of deception is expected to last a lifetime because it is founded on love. Just as one cheers Bud and Fran in their determination to remain incorruptible, one hopes Armbruster and Pamela will continue their masquerade until the final curtain.

8

The Dirty Fairy Tales:
Irma La Douce and *Kiss Me, Stupid*

Irma La Douce (1963)

A FEW MONTHS after *The Apartment* went into nationwide release, *Irma La Douce* opened on Broadway in the fall of 1960 for a run of 526 performances. It was the kind of musical comedy our forefathers would have called "naughty." The title character was a Montmartre prostitute, and her lover was a law student who disguised himself as a rich client, paying her handsomely so she would not share her favors with others. Naturally, one could not believe a word of the plot; and despite the demimondaines parading around the stage, the play was soft at the core. It ended with Irma's giving birth on Christmas Eve.

It was Marguerite Monnot's music-hall score that gave *Irma La Douce* its charm; as often happens, the score redeemed the libretto. In a musical, the score and the book gain and lose as they are made to coalesce. The dialogue gains the embellishment of music, and the music acquires the human context of drama. Music can divert the audience's attention from inconsistency or implausibility; it can also make palatable what might otherwise be offensive. When *Irma La Douce* is revived, it is performed as if it were an operetta; the score is so melodic with its plangent accordion and exuberant xylophone that noboby bats an eyelash at the plot.

When Wilder decided to film *Irma La Douce*, he chose to do it as a straight comedy without songs. His only concession to Marguerite Monnot was to use "Dis-Donc" as a dance number for Shirley MacLaine and reduce the rest of the score to background music. By robbing *Irma* of its score, Wilder was left with a sleazy comedy which he then tried to sentimentalize. In *The Apartment*,

101

Shirley MacLaine romping as the title character in Irma La Douce.

Wilder could combine the sordid and the sentimental because the characters were so palpably real. However, nothing can make *Irma La Douce* realistic because the premise is antirealistic. When a prostitute's lover masquerades as a peer and makes love to his mistress without her knowing his identity, one is really in the world of boulevard comedy and plays like Molnár's *The Guardsman*, where a husband disguises himself as a guardsman and makes love to his own wife. What *Irma* needed was either music or an extremely light touch; Wilder gave it neither.

Quite simply, Wilder wanted to make a gamy movie that would pay off at the box office, as *Irma* did. But it was a gamy movie whose lack of human feeling was evident at the outset. The credits are incorporated into a prologue that opens on a street thronged by prostitutes. Irma stands in a doorway, dressed in a skirt slit up the side, a black sweater, and green stockings; she holds a poodle under her arm. A customer approaches, and they enter the Hotel Casanova. The camera tilts up the facade, and a series of blackout sketches begins, depicting Irma's way of getting more money out of her customers. First, she tells a man how a piano lid ruined her concert career; the customer, obviously moved, drops an extra bill in her purse. Blackout followed by more credits. Irma subjects another customer to a story about her missionary parents and her sister who requires three blood transfusions a day: he also leaves her a generous tip. Finally, a Texan comes along who thinks Irma is only worth five dollars. Thereupon, she reminds him that her orphanage was bombed by American planes; sheepishly, he asks if she takes travelers' checks. Blackout followed by remaining credits.

Wilder was aiming for easy laughs and got them through a series of burlesque skits. But by giving Irma the soul of cash register, he would have a difficult time humanizing her. However, Wilder would do very little humanizing because he had already decided to slant the script in the direction of Irma's lover, Nestor, who assumed a fictitious identity to keep his mistress off the streets. Wilder returned to a theme he had used in *A Foreign Affair*—the innocent who stumbles into an amoral world. First, he changes Nestor from a law student to a policeman. Then, he has Nestor embark on a campaign to clean up Montmartre the way Phoebe Frost took it upon herself to fumigate Berlin. Unfortunately,

Nestor arrests the police inspector and finds himself off the force. Nestor loses his job but wins Irma; but rather than lose Irma to the Rue Casanova, he assumes a disguise. He parts his hair in the middle, pastes on a moustache and a goatee, dons a white eye patch and an ascot, and becomes the mythical Lord X—Irma's one and only protector.

In a film that runs well over two hours, a disguise must be extraordinarily clever to sustain interest. Although Jack Lemmon is a fine comedian, one tires of his switching from Nestor to Lord X. Wilder's interest flagged, also. To jazz up the plot, he resorted to double entendre and movie trivia. But the double entendre is not especially funny because there is no ulterior meaning, only an obvious surface one. When Nestor spots Irma's poodle, Coquette, he says to Irma, "According to the law, you're supposed to keep it on a leash." "On a *leash!*" Irma replies, wide-eyed. Irma takes "it" in the wrong way—which is actually the only way. When Lord X, like Joe in *Some Like It Hot*, feigns impotence, the dialogue assumes the imagery of a gas station. Lord X comments that his tank is dry; Irma replies by telling him about some of her customers who thought they were out of gas but only needed a little push.

Nestor's Lord X is a celluloid creation, pieced together from movie lore. He tells Irma that while he was in a Japanese prison camp, the bridge on the river Kwai (*The Bridge on the River Kwai*, 1957) fell on him, leaving him "half a man." He suffered a detached retina at Navarone (*The Guns of Navarone*, 1961); the silver plate in his elbow is a souvenir of the sinking of the *Bismarck* (*Sink the Bismarck!*, 1960). However, when Nestor suspects that Irma prefers Lord X to himself, he "kills off" the Englishman and is jailed for murder. The phony murder also occurred in the musical, but at that point no one was taking the libretto seriously. However, by casting two naturalistic performers—Jack Lemmon and Shirley MacLaine—in the leads, Wilder was forced into a *cul de sac*; he simply could not wring realism out of fancy. Actually, Wilder did not eviscerate the libretto as cleanly as he should have. In the play, Nestor, discovering that Irma is pregnant, escapes from Devil's Island to be with her. Wilder's Nestor goes to an ordinary prison. At the conclusion of a movie that was overlong to begin with, Wilder starts speeding up the action as if he were undercranking in the tradition of silent comedy. Nestor escapes from prison, disguises himself once more as Lord X to convince the police there was no murder, and marries a visibly pregnant Irma, who goes into labor at the altar and delivers in the sacristy. There is no point elaborating on the monumentally tasteless wedding. But what occurs at the very end is downright exasperating. A figure steps out of a pew and proceeds up the aisle. It is Lord X, complete with eyepatch, umbrella, and homburg. Is one to assume that, unknown to Nestor and Irma, there actually was a Lord X? Clearly, this Lord X is not Nestor in disguise, for Nestor is in the sacristy with Irma and the baby. Is it a joke or a sight gag? Whatever, it is the sort of gimmick Wilder has continually used to conceal a void that, in the original play, was filled by music. Perhaps after a human comedy like *The Apartment*, Wilder was entitled to an inhuman one like *Irma La Douce*. Yet *Kiss Me, Stupid*, his next dirty fairy tale, almost destroyed his reputation as a filmmaker; the irony is that it included the same ingredients that went into *Irma*—disguise, deception, and prostitution—but with people, not puppets, as characters.

Kiss Me, Stupid (1964)

In December 1964, just as the Museum of Modern Art was honoring Wilder with a retrospective, the Legion of Decency was denouncing his latest film, *Kiss Me, Stupid*, for its "crude and suggestive dialogue," "bald condonation of immorality," and "prurient preoccupation with lechery."[1] Oddly enough, the film received the Production Code seal, although the Legion's feelings were shared by many reviewers.

There is no denying that *Kiss Me, Stupid* is frequently gross. The 1960s were a strange period for Wilder. At the beginning and end of the decade, he made two films that rank as touchstones of his art: *The Apartment* and *The Private Life of Sherlock Holmes*. For each film, he had a script that prevented his selling the characters short or reducing them to joke machines. Also, there were no real villains in either film; thus Wilder could not blacken what was only gray. In the quartet of films that followed *The Apartment—One, Two, Three, Irma La Douce, Kiss Me, Stupid*, and *The Fortune Cookie*—Wilder did not have scripts that could temper his cynicism or restrain his penchant for the vulgar. Thus the main characters in those films are far from endearing. In *Kiss Me, Stupid*, they become likable only after an act of deception that involves double adultery. What the Legion of Decency may have been objecting to, without quite knowing how to articulate it, was Wilder's thesis that infidelity can have a humanizing effect, which is rather like saying that the end can justify the means. Still, no matter how common the characters in *Kiss Me, Stupid* are, they are people—not caricatures or musical-comedy stereotypes.

Kiss Me, Stupid, then, is the reverse of *Irma La Douce*—operetta humanized; a soundstage Paris replaced by a real Nevada town where the air is clogged with dust. It is a place where jealousy is not a stock motif but a human emotion; where adultery is not the occasion for blackouts but the means of restoring husband to wife. Like *Irma*, *Kiss Me, Stupid* opens with a credits sequence, but one that is integral to the plot as opposed to a prologue made up of revue skits. Wilder irises in on a Las Vegas decal. Then, as he often does, Wilder moves from the general to the particular; from the Vegas Strip to the marquee of the Sands Hotel announcing its stellar attraction, Dino; and finally from the outside of the hotel to the Copa Room where Dino is crooning "'S Wonderful" and trading wisecracks with the chorus girls. The remaining credits are interspersed with bits from Dino's nightclub act. Dino is none other than Dean Martin; or rather, Dean Martin is playing his persona—the boozy swinger. It was daring of Wilder to give the character Martin's nickname and persona; it was courageous of Martin to accept a role that exploited his image of an amiable but lecherous drunk.

Apart from establishing Dino's character and creating a tawdry mood, the credits sequence also initiates the plot. Instead of staying on in Vegas and juggling dates with jealous chorines, Dino heads for Los Angeles. A detour brings him to Climax, Nevada (puns on the name are inevitable), where he is recognized by an aspiring songwriting team—Barney Millsap (Cliff Osmond), the gas-station owner, and Orville Spooner (Ray Walston), the local piano teacher. To detain Dino long enough to hear their songs, Barney disconnects the fuel line of his car. Dino is forced to stay overnight at the Spooners'. But the pathologically jealous Orville deliberately drives his wife, Zelda (Felicia Farr), out of the house to keep her from being seduced by Dino; and Polly the Pistol (Kim

Novak), a cocktail waitress from a nearby roadhouse, is hired to impersonate Mrs. Spooner for the night.

However, the role becomes the reality. When Dino makes a pass at Polly, Orville throws him out of the house and tenderly takes "Mrs. Spooner" to bed. Meanwhile, the real Mrs. Spooner ends up in Polly's trailer along with the exiled Dino. When Zelda recognizes Dino, she begins plugging her husband's song, "Sophia," which epitomized the kind of rhyming nonsense ("Listen to me, Sophia/Have you any idea/How much you mean to me-A?") that Martin was recording in the 1960s. Later, when Dino sings "Sophia" on network television, Orville is stunned. He looks quizzically at his wife, whose only comment is, "Kiss me, stupid," thereby adding another one-liner to the Wilder collection.

Perhaps it is impossible to convince the skeptics that the film's heart was in the right place; they would argue that Wilder confused the heart with the loins. Yet there is real pathos in *Kiss Me, Stupid*, especially in the scenes with Polly and Orville. Wilder obviously had Marilyn Monroe in mind when he created the character of Polly. Marilyn died in 1962, about two years before the filming of *Kiss Me, Stupid*. In some ways, Polly is Wilder's memorial to Marilyn, who gave her best performances in the two films she made for him. Wilder invested Polly with the same sexy vulnerability that made Marilyn tragic and desirable at the same time. Kim Novak brought a lost-lamb quality to the part; she lacked only the self-mockery of which Marilyn was so capable.

Just as Northrop Frye distinguished between the high and the low mimetic, one might distinguish between the high and the low Lubitsch. *Kiss Me, Stupid* is low Lubitsch. Lubitsch reveled in double entendre, as does Wilder. However, Wilder, unlike his mentor, sometimes confused a double meaning with a dirty joke. Lubitsch would hardly have approved of the exchange between Orville and Polly as he shows her around the house. "It's not very big, but it's clean," Orville notes. "What is?" Polly asks, suspiciously. Nor would Lubitsch have approved of this bit of dialogue between Dino and Orville. "Where am I?" Dino asks, waking from a nap. "In Climax," Orville answers.

Lubitsch always managed to elevate his characters to a level higher than the one they would occupy in real life. The script of *Kiss Me, Stupid* did not allow for much elevating; but it did allow

Ray Walston and Kim Novak on the verge of becoming "Mr. and Mrs. Spooner" in *Kiss Me, Stupid*.

Credit: *Courtesy of Billy Wilder*

for a bit of transfiguring. Wilder was able to idealize Orville and Polly, if only for a short time, by sentimentalizing their relationship. Wilder accomplishes the transfiguration by the Pirandellian trick of the player becoming the part. Orville is at the piano playing Dino a love song that happens to be a forgotten Gershwin number that Wilder resurrected—"All The Livelong Day." The more he plays the song, the more he ceases to be a grubby songwriter and, instead, becomes a protective husband who will not allow his home to be defiled or his wife compromised. After he tosses Dino out of the house, he looks at Polly, speaking to her as if she were his wife. "It's been a long day, hasn't it?" Orville says. "Yes, dear," Polly replies. Orville opens the bedroom door: "Coming, Mrs. Spooner?" The door closes, and the scene slowly fades out. It may not be high Lubitsch, but one suspects the master would have approved.

The same night Polly was playing the wife, Zelda was playing the hooker. Each woman learned something of the other's occupation; each became better for the exchange of roles. The trailer scene between Dino and Zelda is also low Lubitsch (one cannot imagine a Lubitsch couple in a trailer), but done with as much subtlety as the situation would allow. Zelda, clad in a robe, gazes at the sleeping Dino and muses on what might have happened if he weren't asleep and she weren't old-fashioned. Fade out and in on Zelda fast asleep and Dino departing, after leaving five hundred dollars in an empty scotch bottle—presumably for services rendered. Zelda awakens; she is clearly nude. What happened to the robe she was wearing in the previous scene? Did they or didn't they?

Kiss Me, Stupid was Wilder's contribution to "bed trick" comedy in which one woman takes another's place in bed. Shakespeare was not above using the bed trick in *Measure for Measure*, where Mariana stood in for Isabella; nor was Hugo von Hofmannsthal in his libretto for Richard Strauss's opera *Arabella*, in which Zdenka substituted for her sister. Significantly, both *Measure for Measure* and *Arabella* are set in Vienna, which clearly has an edge on Climax, Nevada. Had Wilder set *Kiss Me, Stupid* in the Vienna of Maria Theresa with a soundtrack of recycled Strauss, it might have offended fewer people.

As it happened, Wilder came upon an Italian bedroom farce, Anna Bonacci's *L'Ora della Fantasia* (The Hour of Fantasy),[2] in which George Sedley, an organist in an English village, dreams about becoming a composer-conductor. When a friend hears that Sir Ronald, a high-ranking magistrate, will be passing through the village, he arranges for Sir Ronald to spend the night at the Sedleys.' George regards Sir Ronald's presence in his home as a means of furthering his musical career and of making himself and his wife, Mary, Lord and Lady Sedley. When George discovers that Sir Ronald is a notorious womanizer, he hires Geraldine, the local prostitute, to impersonate his wife, who is to be ensconced at Geraldine's house for the night. But man and mask merge; George and Geraldine begin speaking to each other as husband and wife. When Sir Ronald compromises Geraldine, George ejects him from the house and takes his "wife" to bed.

Meanwhile, Sir Ronald goes over to Geraldine's house, where one expects the inevitable to take place. But, after teasing Sir Ronald, Mary Sedley finally reveals her identity. Sir Ronald begs

her for one hour of fantasy. As she is about to leave, he calls her by
the name of Mrs. Sedley; she does not respond. Then he calls her
Geraldine; this time, she does. Sir Ronald gets his one hour of
fantasy; Geraldine gets a preview of married life; Mary gets to be
whore for a night; and George gets his oratorio performed in
London.

In adapting the play, Wilder changed the names of the characters, transferred the setting from rural England to the American
Southwest, and deleted the pretentious dialogue about illusion and
reality. Yet he kept the play's paradoxical thesis that certain forms
of deception can benefit people spiritually by giving them the
human dimension they have been lacking; and materially, by
fulfilling their dreams.

An early screenplay, *Music in the Air* (1934), helped Wilder
make further changes in Bonacci's play. Sedley and his friend
Taylor become the frustrated songwriters, Orville Spooner and
Barney Millsap. *Music in the Air* also included a songwriting team
and centered around the composer's efforts to get his song "I've
Told Ev'ry Little Star" published. Both films have similar endings:
Music in the Air ends with the composer's hearing his song over the
air; *Kiss Me, Stupid*, with Orville's hearing Dino sing "Sophia" on
television.

There is a moral to the *Kiss Me, Stupid* controversy: last year's
shocker may be this year's "Early Show." In 1970, United Artists—
the company that, six years earlier, refused to release *Kiss Me,
Stupid* and turned it over to its subsidiary, Lopert Pictures, for U.S.
distribution—re-released the film with what was then called a GP
(All Ages Admitted; Parental Guidance Suggested) rating; today,
the letters are transposed—PG. *Kiss Me, Stupid* now joins the ranks
of *The Moon Is Blue* (1953), *The Man with the Golden Arm* (1955),
and *Never on Sunday* (1960)—scandals in their time, innocuous
television fare today.

9

Bosom Buddies: *The Fortune Cookie* and *The Front Page*

WILDER BEGAN EXPLORING the nature of male friendship in *Double Indemnity* a quarter of a century before George Roy Hill revived the buddy film with *Butch Cassidy and the Sundance Kid* (1969). In the relationship between Neff and Keyes, Wilder caught the way American males reveal their affection for each other—with an "I love you" inflected like a wisecrack. Only at the end do the words revert to their literal meaning in an admission of love that is mutual. In the films that followed *Double Indemnity*, Wilder continued to depict the various ways males express their feelings toward each other: hero worship (Herbie and Tatum in *The Big Carnival*, Cookie and Sefton in *Stalag 17*); paternalism (Colonel Plummer and Pringle in *A Foreign Affair*); domestic unions where the men behave like married couples (Joe and Jerry in *Some Like It Hot*, Holmes and Watson in *The Private Life of Sherlock Holmes*). On the other hand, relationships between brothers are strained in Wilder's films; his brothers are such opposites that neither can understand the other (Don and Wick in *The Lost Weekend*, Linus and David in *Sabrina*, Holmes and Mycroft in *The Private Life of Sherlock Holmes*). Don, Linus, and Holmes need women who combine feminine warmth with fraternal affection. Don gravitates to Helen, the Good Joe type; Linus to Sabrina, Peter Pan in basic black; and Holmes to the mysterious Gabrielle.

The Fortune Cookie (1966)

In *The Fortune Cookie*, brothers-in-law fare worse than brothers; there are not even any female buddies around to serve as ideal mates. When Wilder conceived the idea for *The Fortune Cookie*,

111

he was still in his *Kiss Me, Stupid* frame of mind; he had not completely soured on mankind but still felt that only a chosen few, the eternal naifs, could crack the iron cocoon of the self. The price of integrity is high; two against the world are two in isolation. Thus *The Apartment* ends with Bud and Fran playing gin rummy in a virtually empty apartment; *The Fortune Cookie*, with two men tossing a football on a deserted gridiron. Both couples will enjoy a rich life; but it is a life that only the pure of heart, that blessed minority, will appreciate.

Significantly, the incorruptibles in *The Fortune Cookie* are two males: a television cameraman, Harry Hinkle (Jack Lemmon), and a black football player, Boom-Boom Jackson (Ron Rich), a latter-day Huck Finn and Tom Sawyer, whose basic decency contrasts sharply with the mendacity of Harry's estranged wife, Sandy (Judi West), and his brother-in-law, Willie (Walter Matthau). Wilder is retelling *The Apartment*, this time from the male point of view and from a dual perspective where the action is seen misanthropically and sentimentally. He has chosen a difficult method; it requires the filmmaker to adopt a Janus persona and coordinate what both eyes see—the jaundiced eye as well as the healthy one. However, Wilder's vision was not twenty-twenty when he made *The Fortune Cookie*, as it was when he made *The Apartment*. Then, he could collapse both profiles into a full face because the characters were not unregenerate. But there are villains in *The Fortune Cookie* who are beyond salvation; and the heroes are like Kilroy in Tennessee Williams's *Camino Real*—grown men with hearts as big as a baby's head.

Although Wilder plays favorites in *The Fortune Cookie*, he feigns objectivity with an impersonal structure. He divides the film into sixteen sequences, each with its own catchy title ("The Legal Eagles," "The Return of Tinker Bell," "The Gemini Plan," etc.); the overall effect recalls the old movie serials where the plot unfolded in weekly chapters, each of which was provocatively titled. In fact, *The Fortune Cookie* opens in an unabashedly old-fashioned way; the credits appear, white on black, to the music of "You'd Be So Nice to Come Home To," orchestrated with a lush Big Band sound. Structurally, *The Fortune Cookie* harks back to the classic kind of screenwriting where the cords of the plot were knotted at select

points, so that when the unraveling began, the nodes could loosen
one by one.

In the first nine sequences, Wilder stretches the narrative line as
tautly as he can, knowing exactly where to knot it. While
photographing a football game between the Cleveland Browns
and the Minnesota Vikings, Hinkle collides with Boom-Boom and
is hurled across the sideline. Hinkle's brother-in-law, Willie, a
shyster lawyer who works out of a cubicle that resembles the Old
Curiosity Shop, decides to capitalize on Harry's nonexistent
injuries and sue CBS, the Browns, and Cleveland Municipal
Stadium for $1 million. Because Boom-Boom believes Harry may
be paralyzed, he keeps a vigil at the hospital, sends flowers, and
even buys him a battery-operated wheelchair. When Harry is
released from the hospital, Boom-Boom becomes his manservant.
With sequence 10, Wilder ties another knot; Harry's estranged wife
arrives, presumably to care for her invalid husband but actually to
get her share of the insurance money for a nightclub act. In the last
sequence, Wilder initiates the slackening process by using one
incident to unravel the knotty complications caused by Willie's
scheme. A racial slur against Boom-Boom so infuriates Harry that
he exposes the hoax, literally kicks Sandy out of the house, and
seeks out the only person who has not sunk into the bogs of greed—
Boom-Boom.

When Boom-Boom sees that Harry is mobile, he realizes the
accident was a fraud. Yet their friendship is too pure to be sullied
by Willie's machinations. Instead of a spoken admission of guilt
and a speech of forgiveness, the men toss a football back and forth.
Boom-Boom tackles Harry, throwing him to the ground. This time,
it seems that Harry has suffered a real injury; but he opens his eyes
and breaks into a grin. The men continue their game, having
learned that life is more often a matter of tossing the ball to another
than running with it alone.

To glorify the relationship between Boom-Boom and Harry,
Wilder portrays the other characters as total reprobates. Willie,
who makes his living by turning whiplash cases into million-dollar
lawsuits, regards his brother-in-law as nothing more than material
for another insurance caper. As played by Walter Matthau, Willie is
not just abrasive; he has a soul of sandpaper. The women are
callous and self-seeking. Feigning concern, Sandy calls Harry from

New York while she is with another man. She is a typical super-vixen; after six months, she has only reached page nineteen of *The Carpetbaggers*. When Sandy arrives in Cleveland, she senses a rival in Boom-Boom; she mocks his loyalty and criticizes his cooking, offering to make Harry one of her inedible meatloaves to counteract the effects of Boom-Boom's chicken paprika.

Boom-Boom is really Harry's double; he is truly a black brother. Neither man was meant for women, for each of them only attracts cheats and hookers. To emphasize the affinity that exists between Harry and Boom-Boom, Wilder pairs each of them with a blonde gold digger—Harry with Sandy, and Boom-Boom with a black girl with dyed blonde hair who slides up to him in a bar. He is so repelled by her vamp act that he tells her escort to take her home and dunk her head in a pot of ink. Both men loathe the same thing—fraud, whether it is a black woman's simulating the look of a blonde Venus or a wife's affecting conjugal love to get her share of the insurance money.

Although Wilder constructs the film so that it favors Harry and Boom-Boom, he does not immediately set up a bipolar structure where the two stand out in moral and visual contrast to everyone else. He builds their friendship on the ashes of burned-out relationships, slowly elevating their camaraderie into an ideal union. Furthermore, Wilder does it visually as well as dramatically. Boom-Boom usually remains in the background, like Cookie in *Stalag 17*; he is rarely in a prominent part of the frame. When he moves to Harry's apartment, he continues to occupy a subservient role. When Harry tells Boom-Boom about Sandy, Harry is in the left of the frame; Boom-Boom is in the back, leaning against a table by the window. When Harry joyously circles the floor in his wheelchair, Boom-Boom withdraws to the back of the room. As Boom-Boom moves from manservant to friend, he advances to the foreground, finally sharing the frame with Harry as Wilder freezes their faces into a still—two boy men, another odd couple like Bud and Fran, refusing to trade their integrity for easy money.

The purity of male camaraderie so fascinated Wilder that he planned to make it the basis of his next film, *The Private Life of Sherlock Holmes*. In interviews, Wilder was quite explicit about his view of the bond between Holmes and Watson. They were a male couple like Colonel Pickering and Henry Higgins in Shaw's

Pygmalion, sometimes testy and irritable but unswervingly devoted to each other. Wilder envisioned a male love story that would also be a valentine to Conan Doyle. As it happened, the projected love story became a tale of Holmes's unsatisfied love for a woman who combined a smoldering femininity with a formidable intelligence—a woman who would have been the perfect wife-mistress-friend, had she lived. In *Avanti!* love became possible again; but it was not the love of devoted friends or moonstruck innocents, but a realistic love between a married man and a plucky girl who, realizing that life involves compromises, decide that an annual summer holiday together is better than nothing.

Once a theme finds its way into Wilder's consciousness, it enters his catalog of plot devices and starts recurring in subsequent films. The latest Wilder movie will often incorporate themes from the ones preceding it. The melodrama of *Five Graves to Cairo* spilled over into *Double Indemnity*; the mild cynicism of *A Foreign Affair* grew stronger in *Sunset Boulevard* and permeated *The Big Carnival*. One would therefore expect *The Front Page* to repeat themes from the films that preceded it—namely, friendship between men, love between men and woman, and the inevitable contrast.

The Front Page (1974)

It was natural that Wilder should have a try at *The Front Page*, the Ben Hecht–Charles MacArthur newspaper comedy that, since its premiere in 1928, has gone on to become a minor American classic. Wilder knew the newspaper world, as he demonstrated in *The Big Carnival*; he also understood media, as he showed in such films as *Sunset Boulevard*, *The Spirit of St. Louis*, and *The Fortune Cookie*. If anyone could capture life in a press room, Wilder could. The Hecht-MacArthur play also afforded him another opportunity to depict male friendship; not the classic or sacred type between a Harry Hinkle and a Boom-Boom Jackson, but the more profane and familiar kind where a friend becomes an old shoe—easy to step into and sometimes on. In short, it would be the type Wilder portrayed in *Some Like It Hot*, where the friends compete with each other, scheme against each other, but do not sever the ties that keep them together because mutual need is more important than personal pride.

The Front Page is the most faithful of Wilder's adaptations. Inevitably, he made changes: Peggy is an organist at a movie theater; Bensinger is outrageously effeminate; and the attempt to kidnap Peggy's mother is omitted. But Wilder did retain the play's double plot, which paralleled an editor's efforts to keep his star reporter from getting married with a prostitute's attempt to save her anarchist boyfriend from the gallows. However, what is truly unusual about the film is the fact that, without altering the plot, Wilder transformed the play into a screwball comedy featuring not the battle of the sexes but an ongoing battle between two members of the same sex.

There was little about the original *Front Page* to suggest the topsy-turvy world of screwball. Nor was the first film version that Lewis Milestone directed in 1931 a true screwball comedy. Screwball turns the world on its ear; smartly dressed men and women outwit each other; the virile hero (ex-husband, rejected suitor) sabotages the heroine's love life and prevents her from marrying a milquetoast; the sassy heroine (ex-wife, former fiancée) saves the hero from marrying into a family of stuffy bluebloods.

To create a screwball comedy from a play about an editor who will do anything to keep his ace reporter, one can (a) change the reporter's sex, so that the editor wants *her* for both the paper and himself; (b) complicate the scenario by making the reporter the editor's ex-wife, now engaged to a humorless insurance executive who wants to take her from the dull world of journalism to swinging Albany; and (c) collapse the triangle (man/woman/rival) into a straight line at whose extremities stand man and woman, facing each other in the most archetypal of battles—the battle of the sexes. What has just been described is Howard Hawks's film version of *The Front Page, His Girl Friday* (1940). Hawks's transformation worked perfectly. Hildy Johnson is an ambisexual name; it was the reporter's name in the original play, where Hildy was played by Lee Tracy; it was the reporter's name in the first movie version, where Hildy was played by Pat O'Brien. But Hildy could also be a woman's name, and Howard Hawks's

Men playing games: Walter Burns (Walter Matthau) and Hildy Johnson (Jack Lemmon) in *The Front Page.*

Credit: Margaret Herrick Library

Hildy Johnson was a lady reporter played by one of the screen's legendary ladies—Rosalind Russell.

However, Wilder kept Hildy a male and still managed to make a screwball comedy by emphasizing a common occurrence in male friendships—a woman's disruptive presence. The conflict between Hildy (Jack Lemmon) and his editor Walter Burns (Walter Matthau) is really a romantic conflict because it is essentially a scheme to eliminate a rival—namely, Hildy's fiancée, Peggy. It is also a type of conflict that is rooted in jealousy; the jealous lover knows that he/she has more to offer the beloved than the rival. Thus the sex of lover, beloved, and rival is irrelevant; what is significant is the confrontation, the agon, the sexual sparring, and the fusillades of wit. Some critics have found a homosexual aura hanging over Wilder's films about males.[1] There is about as much homosexuality in *The Front Page* as there is in the Yankees' dugout. Wilder is spoofing sexual stereotypy again by making Walter Matthau and Jack Lemmon—two actors whose masculinity only a spiteful eunuch would question—the aggressive lover and the unsuspecting beloved of screwball.

Yet Wilder is also making a realistic film that must conform to his standards of realism. *Mise-en-scène* must define time and place; the shots must be visual transcriptions of the script. *The Front Page*, then, is realistic screwball; a point Wilder makes at the outset when the credits appear as type is being set to ragtime. A newspaper comes to life, but according to the headline—June 6, 1929—it is a newspaper of another time; a time when criminals were hanged, as the gallows in the courtyard below the press room makes plain. Wilder is back in Chicago, the Chicago of the St. Valentine's Day Massacre, the Chicago of *Some Like It Hot*; in fact, he is back in the same year—1929—and the same madcap world; tender and tough, gritty and gilded.

Everything about Wilder's *mise-en-scène* evokes the newspaper business. Burns's office is glass-enclosed, and through the panes, reporters are seen busily answering phones and banging out copy. They speak in the vernacular. Wilder availed himself of the new freedom of speech, but just enough to stay within the boundaries of PG. "I'll bury my shoe up your ass!" Hildy warns his editor. Wilder stops short of the national obscenity—which, in 1974, would have meant an automatic R—and instead uses its weaker form, "frig." "Am I glad to get out of this friggin' town!" Hildy exclaims. In trying to update the language, Wilder sometimes uses references (Burns tells Peggy that Hildy is a "flasher") and idioms ("getting it up," "kicking in balls") that are jarringly anachronistic.

But this is screwball; so one accepts, however grudgingly, a few anachronisms including a Freudian psychologist who interprets a gun as a phallic symbol; and television's own Carol Burnett, badly miscast as the prostitute Molly Malloy. A screwball comedy should have a true screwball—a dizzy dame, a runaway heiress, a hobo who is really a millionaire. Wilder makes the anarchist, Earl Williams (Austin Pendleton), the screwball of *The Front Page*.

In neither film version was Earl particularly memorable; all one can recall of John Qualen's performance in *His Girl Friday* was a visionary fervor that soon grew tiresome. Wilder built up the part for Austin Pendleton, who played Earl charmingly, as if he were a campus bookworm en route to the library and, by mistake, wandered into an antiwar rally where he was radicalized on the spot. The first time one sees Earl, he is handcuffed, his nose running. A kindly policeman wipes his nose for him, and the two talk matter-of-factly about summer colds. To make Earl even more likable, Wilder turns him into a baker who puts "Free Sacco and Vanzetti" slips into fortune cookies. Earl, like Wilder, has little use for Freudians. "He's crazy!" Earl remarks when Dr. Eggelhoffer asks if he practices self-abuse.

Molly's selfless love for Earl is the exact opposite of Burns's manipulative affection for Hildy. Molly loves Earl so much that she risks death by jumping out of a window to distract Bensinger from opening the roll-top desk where Earl is hiding. Conversely, Burns needs Hildy so badly that he wrecks Hildy's marriage with a lie that is one of the most celebrated curtain lines in theater history. Despite Burns's machinations, one has no doubt that he has real feeling for Hildy. But Burns is incapable of purity of intention; that is reserved for the pure of heart—for Bud and Fran, for Earl and his Molly.

Like the lover who alone knows what is best for the beloved, Burns knows what is best for Hildy; and it is not marriage. However, it seems that Burns will not be able to stop the wedding. Hildy and Peggy are headed for Philadelphia. Burns is at the station, seeing them off. Visually, he is excluded from their lives. Burns stands on the platform, watching Hildy's reconciliation with Peggy through the train window. In a touching gesture of apology, Hildy kisses Peggy's hand. After the train pulls out, Burns saunters over to the telegraph office at the end of the platform and asks the operator to wire ahead to the police at the next stop. "The son of a bitch stole my watch," he explains.

For the optimists who think Hildy managed to escape from Burns's clutches, Wilder has added a "What Happened to Whom" epilogue with pictures of the characters on the right and their whereabouts on the left—rather like an alumni newsletter, only wittier. Burns retired from the *Examiner* and joined the faculty of the University of Chicago as a lecturer in ethics; Hildy became editor; Earl and Molly married; and Peggy also married—not Hildy, but a nephew of Leopold Stokowski. In case anyone wonders what happened to Dr. Eggelhoffer, he returned to Vienna after Earl accidentally shot him in the groin and wrote *The Joys of Impotence.*

Lewis Milestone's *The Front Page* ended with Burns and Hildy facing each other with an ambiguous THE END? in the center of the frame. Wilder answered any questions with a screwball epilogue, to which we might make a screwball addendum. When Hildy retired from the *Examiner* as an inveterate bachelor, he joined his former boss at the University of Chicago, where they team taught Business Ethics.

10

The Misfires: *The Emperor Waltz* and *The Spirit of St. Louis*

CRITICALLY, Wilder's films fall into three categories: classics (e.g., *Double Indemnity, Some Like It Hot, The Apartment*); *films maudits*, box-office failures that were lukewarmly reviewed but, upon reevaluation, have gained in respect and popularity (*The Big Carnival, The Private Life of Sherlock Holmes, Avanti!*); and miscalculations (*The Emperor Waltz, The Spirit of St. Louis*) that tell one more about Wilder than they do about his art. One would hardly think of Wilder as a Fourth-of-July American, but he is; one would doubt that he believes in God, but he does. *The Emperor Waltz* expressed his belief in America; *The Spirit of St. Louis*, his belief in a Supreme Being.

Yankee Doodle Billy

Born Samuel and nicknamed Billy because of his mother's affection for Buffalo Bill, Wilder was a spiritual American since childhood. America meant Buffalo Bill's Wild West Show, Tom Mix, chewing gum, Cream of Wheat, and especially jazz. Throughout his youth and early manhood, Wilder was constantly witnessing the impact of American culture on European life. When he came to Paramount in 1937, his first assignment was to convert *Champagne Waltz*, a scenario he had written about the effect of American jazz on the musical taste of Vienna, into a screenplay. Wilder's script was never used, and he only received story credit for *Champagne Waltz* (1937). But there was enough of Wilder in the plot to indicate that the new screenwriters had not radically altered the original story line in which a swing band, Buzzy Bellew and His Musical Crew, is booked next door to the Viennese Waltz Palace, whose bubbly fare cannot compete with *le jazz hot*. Bellew

123

Man Alone: James Stewart as Charles Lindbergh in The Spirit of St. Louis.

Credit: Movie Star News

falls in love with Elsa Strauss, the waltz queen; but because she
regards jazz as lowbrow, Bellew is forced to conceal his identity
and masquerade first as a consul and later as an icebox salesman.
However, jazz and the waltz can coexist; and to prove it, the
orchestra from the Waltz Palace crosses the Atlantic and converts
America to music in three-quarter time.

Champagne Waltz was a failure, but Wilder had not forgotten
the "American in Vienna" theme. After finishing *The Lost Weekend*, he started work on *The Emperor Waltz*, converting the jazz
musician and the waltz queen of *Champagne Waltz* into the
commoner and the blueblood of operetta. The commoner would
be Virgil Smith, a phonograph salesman from Newark, who travels
to Vienna to interest Emperor Franz Josef in his product; the
blueblood, the Countess Johanna whom he woos and wins in the
bargain.

The Emperor Waltz (1948)

Everything about *The Emperor Waltz* pointed to a sure-fire hit.
The casting seemed perfect: Bing Crosby as Virgil and Joan
Fontaine as the Countess. The film would be photographed in
Technicolor, a process that Paramount used sparingly in the 1940s.
Paramount Technicolor had a soft, muted quality, unlike MGM's
hot rainbow look. Thus Paramount's color photography could give
Franz Josef's court an appearance that was mellow but not
overripe. Furthermore, *The Emperor Waltz* would be a comedy
with music—like Lubitsch's *Monte Carlo* or *One Hour with You*—
where Bing Crosby would warble "I Kiss Your Hand, Madame"
and serenade Joan Fontaine with a song that, to many, is the
quintessence of operetta: "Une chambre separée," freely translated in the movie as "The Kiss in Your Eyes."

In a Paramount musical, the songs were worked into the plot, as
distinguished from the MGM type, closer to true musical comedy,
where the plot was worked around the production numbers. Thus
Wilder would not have to subordinate his script to the score. In
addition, *The Emperor Waltz* would give Wilder his first opportunity to film in color. He chose yellow as the perfect color for
capturing the sunset of the Austro-Hungarian Empire. The film
opens with the credits on yellow brocade as the soundtrack evokes

turn-of-the-century Vienna with the title waltz. Gilt is everywhere; golden light glazes the windows, and even the fade outs are yellow. It would seem that Wilder was really making a Lubitsch film. But what went wrong?

Steamed Clams and Sacher Torte

The clue is in the printed prologue that informs us we are at one of the Emperor's "little clambakes." From yellow brocade to steamers, it appears. It may seem picayune to criticize Wilder for resorting to slang to get an easy laugh (although calling a ball a clambake is hardly funny); yet the prologue crystallizes what is wrong with the film: Wilder was unable to sustain the mood he so delicately established during the credits. Furthermore, he resorts to a double "meet-cute" on the assumption that if a romance between a salesman and a countess is cute, one between their dogs is cuter. Perhaps Wilder thought that a canine microcosm within a human macrocosm was Lubitschian. It is true that in Lubitsch's *Monte Carlo*, the heroine attends an operetta in which the stage action mirrors events in her own life; thus, the theater becomes a microcosm of reality as art begins to imitate life. However, making the theater a mirror of reality is quite different from making puppy love a metaphor for human courtship.

Wilder did not trust his material the way Lubitsch did. Lubitsch was able to spoof the conventions of operetta because, basically, he respected operetta; he accepted it as a valid type of musical theater employing certain unrealistic elements to achieve its end which was a blend of lighthearted song and light-headed story. A believer in the world of operetta has certain privileges that are denied the agnostic. He can spoof that world, for spoofing—as opposed to satirizing—is born of respect; it is a harmless game the lover plays on the beloved, as whimsical and ultimately as charming as the way Chagall makes lovers airborne and giddy without demeaning them.

However, Wilder is a realist; while he enjoys using the plot devices of operetta, particularly disguise and deception, he prefers them in a realistic context, not in a never-never land where duets are sung over the telephone. But *The Emperor Waltz* was not planned as a straight masquerade like *Midnight* or *The Major and the Minor*; it was conceived as an operetta that could only have been made by a person who was sympathetic to a form that was even more unrealistic than opera.

Unfortunately, Wilder was not that person; thus he could only achieve Lubitschian moments, such as the opening when Virgil climbs up the terrace of the imperial palace. The camera accompanies him, tracking in through the window and remaining on the balcony to observe the waltzing couples below. But such moments are few because Wilder's sympathies are not with the Viennese royalty but with the American salesman and his dog, Buttons. Virgil is a Wilder portrait. Both Wilder and his fictional creation knew the frustrations involved in peddling a product; Virgil encounters snobs who not only think salesmen are vulgar but also their wares, especially phonographs; by his own admission, Wilder dragged his carcass up and down Hollywood Boulevard for over a year before he sold an original story.

Instead of being a frilly valentine to Vienna, *The Emperor Waltz* became a stars-and-stripes salute to America. American know-how surpasses the impractical baroque. "You [Americans] are simpler; you are stronger. Ultimately, the world will be yours," the Emperor admiringly says to Virgil. If this sounds jingoistic, one should remember that Wilder, who spent his youth in Vienna, regards the day in 1939, when he became an American citizen, as one of the most significant in his life.

Not only are resilient Americans superior to the decadent Viennese, but their mutts are superior to pedigreed poodles. The Emperor wants Johanna's poodle, Scheherazade, to mate with one of his dogs; but the poodle cannot accommodate just anybody. Wilder indulges his bias against psychiatry by having Scheherazade psychoanalyzed by one of Freud's former pupils. To put it delicately, the poodle is "tense"; and only with Virgil's mutt, Buttons, does her anxiety abate. In fact, it abates to such a degree that she swims across a lake to the music of the *William Tell* Overture to be with Buttons. The Buttons-Scheherazade romance eclipses the one between Virgil and Johanna. When Scheherazade becomes a mother, the wicked baron plans to destroy her litter because it was sired by a mongrel. But Virgil comes to the rescue, eager to end class distinctions on all levels including the canine.

In operetta, there is usually a double pairing off at the end: hero and heroine, and the supporting leads (valet and lady in waiting, the duenna and the crusty old bachelor, etc.). But in *The Emperor Waltz* the supporting leads are the dogs who have rather perversely and inconsiderately consummated their union before Virgil and Johanna. Obviously, they knew they were the true stars of the movie. Thus, instead of being a true operetta, *The Emperor Waltz* became an envoi to a world that was synonymous with operetta. For all its yellow brocade and gold trim, the true color scheme of *The Emperor Waltz* is red, white, and blue.

The Spirit of St. Louis (1957)

It was patriotism, but of a different sort, that also prompted *The Spirit of St. Louis*. Lindbergh was one of Wilder's heroes, and with the advent of widescreen, the mid-1950s seemed the right time for a movie about Lindbergh's transatlantic flight. 1957 was also the right year, for it would mark the thirtieth anniversary of the historic flight. Although Wilder could work comfortably with Cinema-Scope, the material was wrong for him. William Wellman could make aviation films, and Ernst Lubitsch could make operettas; Billy Wilder excelled at neither.

Yet, like *The Emperor Waltz, The Spirit of St. Louis* opens auspiciously; an airplane soars into the wild blue yonder to the music of Franz Waxman's noble prelude with its fragments of the *Marseillaise*. The credits appear against the sky, and a simple prologue follows. It is the morning of May 20, 1927. Lindbergh is asleep in the Garden City Hotel; the lobby is thronged with reporters, most of whom are the newshounds that are so common in Wilder's films. A phonograph is playing "Rio Rita," and Lindy begins to reminisce.

Realizing that it would be impossible to generate much drama from the more than thirty-three hours Lindbergh spent in the air, Wilder resorted to a technique that worked so well in *Double Indemnity*—flashbacks with voice-over narration. However, the *Double Indemnity* flashbacks, apart from being integral to the plot, were dramatically interesting; those in *Spirit* fill up the time between takeoff and landing. They also tend to be reminiscences rather than memories; and with James Stewart as Lindbergh, they become meandering reminiscences.

The best movie flashbacks have always been motivated, as an event of the present evoked an event of the past. Only occasionally do past and present interlock in *Spirit*. Lindbergh's need for sleep occasions a flashback to his boyhood, when he was constantly dozing off, even while fishing; the sight of a St. Christopher medal hanging over the controls turns the clock back to the time he tried to teach a priest how to fly. Sometimes the connections are logical but unimaginative. Lindbergh looks out the plane window, spotting a man on a motorcycle. "I had a motorcycle once," he recalls; flashback to the day he traded in his motorcycle for a plane. But the flashbacks are mostly segments of the past worked into the present like pieces of a jigsaw puzzle that are made to form the right picture no matter how awkwardly they fit.

Stewart's voice-over narration was another problem. Fred Mac-Murray's voice was not eccentric; Stewart's was. Stewart never had an exemplary screen voice, although it fit the guileless characters he portrayed in *Mr. Smith Goes to Washington* (1939) and *It's a Wonderful Life* (1946). But Stewart never had to narrate an entire film before. *Spirit* revealed a voice without nuance that, in moments of emotion, tended to be raspy and strident.

The old devices were not working; now, even words failed Wilder. In *Spirit*, one waits for a Wilder line, a zinger that leaves a spoor of acid behind, the epigram destined for the annals of movie quotations. But the dialogue is telegraphically sparse: "Fog. One hour from St. John's. Fog. Maybe it's only a patch hanging from the mountains." Maybe it is; unfortunately, one does not care.

Lacking the right kind of dialogue to advance the plot, Wilder relied on images. On a visual level, *Spirit* is by no means embarrassing. Wilder's visual sense never leaned toward the painterly or the iconographic; it was story telling through images that sprang directly from the action—Lindbergh parachuting from his mail plane into a swirl of snow; the *Spirit* breaking out of a casement of fog into a welcoming sunset; a sky festooned with multicolored balloons during a flying circus show.

The takeoff preparations are not a series of statically composed shots; they are pictorial drama—"moving pictures" in the literal sense. At dawn, the *Spirit* is towed ceremoniously along a dirt runway wet with rain. As the spectators crowd around the *Spirit*, Wilder brings them into the action, shooting through the plane window to include their faces with Lindbergh's. The actual takeoff is done in classic montage: quick cuts of the rear of the plane, then a close-up of Lindbergh; a long shot of the *Spirit* followed by one of the spectators; a subjective tracking shot of the runway that puts the viewer in the cockpit; and the majestic finale as the *Spirit* soars over the telephone wires that almost ensnare it.

The imagery of the landing is equally dramatic. From the air, Paris resembles a brilliantly lit parade ground. The *Spirit* passes over the Arch of Triumph and the Eiffel Tower as it heads toward Le Bourget. Suddenly, the propellers spin into the frame, and the crowd roars. The sequence was wordless except for Lindbergh's brief prayer: "O God, help me." These words are followed by a shot of the St. Christopher medal at the controls. As the French cheer their hero, Wilder cuts back to the medal, enabling it to share in the applause.

Religious objects can be embarrassing if they are pietistic talismans or symbols of a character's innate goodness. One still winces when the rosary drops out of Helen Hayes's hand in *My Son John* (1952). But the St. Christopher medal is not an emotional ploy; it is an integral part of the plot and, as such, deserves to be the film's climactic image. Lindbergh finally accepts what the medal represents: a belief in a higher power whose existence he had previously doubted.

The St. Christopher medal is not the only instance of Wilder's love of objects; *Spirit* contains the most poignant use of his favorite prop—the mirror. Just before takeoff, Lindbergh discovers he needs a mirror to read the magnetic compass. A woman who has traveled from Philadelphia to witness the event offers him her pocket mirror. Later, when she is on the train back to Philadelphia, she rummages in her purse for her mirror. At first, she is puzzled when she cannot find it; but when she realizes where it is, her face glows with pride. She finds her reflection in a piece of chromium by the window and puts on her lipstick.

Calling *Spirit* a noble attempt praises it and damns it at the same time. It has the worst feature of a noble movie: lovely to look at but frequently dull. Takeoff and landing are visually exciting, but these are only two sequences in a film that runs over two hours. Thanks to television, *Spirit* has a wider audience than it did when it was released in the spring of 1957. In May 1977, it was telecast for the first time to commemorate the fiftieth anniversary of Lindbergh's flight; it now seems on the verge of becoming an annual event, the way World War II films show up on the tube around the anniversaries of Pearl Harbor and D-day.

However, it is doubtful that either *The Emperor Waltz* or *The Spirit of St. Louis* will find favor with the revisionists. Biographically, they deserve attention for what they reveal about the director, who, in one film, converted a monarch to democracy and, in another, gave the final shot to a St. Christopher medal and made the last words a prayer. Therefore, one should not be surprised to discover that Billy Wilder—the man William Holden once described as having a "brain full of razor blades"—begins each script with the letters CD—an abbreviation for *Cum Deo*, Latin for "With God."

11

Sleuthing Around: *Witness for the Prosecution* and *The Private Life of Sherlock Holmes*

THE 1950s were a prolific decade for Wilder; of the nine films he made during that period, four were adaptations of Broadway hits. As one adaptation was finished, another was waiting in the wings. Paramount released *Stalag 17* during the summer of 1953, a few months before *Sabrina Fair* opened in New York. When Wilder was shooting *Sabrina* in the fall of 1953, *The Seven Year Itch* was enjoying a successful New York engagement. When the movie version of *The Seven Year Itch* premiered in the summer of 1955, Agatha Christie's *Witness for the Prosecution* was attracting capacity audiences on Broadway.

One can understand Wilder's attraction to comedies like *Sabrina Fair* and *The Seven Year Itch*; but *Witness for the Prosecution* seemed more suited to Hitchcock's talents than to Wilder's. Adapting a piece of crime fiction like *Double Indemnity* was one thing; filming a British courtroom melodrama—much less one with a plot twist so unusual that audiences were requested not to divulge it—was something else. Certainly Christie's twist, in which the defendant's wife assumed a self-incriminating disguise to free her guilty husband from a murder charge, must have fascinated Wilder. But *Witness for the Prosecution* would not merely be a mask-donning movie. There was another reason for Wilder's attraction to a play written by the mistress of detection; namely, his long-standing interest in the master of detection, Arthur Conan Doyle, and his creation Sherlock Holmes.

At the same time that Wilder was filming *Witness for the Prosecution* in the summer of 1957, he was planning to produce a Broadway musical about Sherlock Holmes. Two years earlier, he received permission from the Conan Doyle estate to do so, after promising Adrian Conan Doyle, the author's son, that he would not

133

The Private Life of Sherlock Holmes: *Holmes (Robert Stephens), Gabrielle-Ilsa (Genevieve Page), and Dr. Watson (Colin Blakely), under surveillance of German agents disguised as monks.*

Credit: *Movie Star News*

parody his father's creation. The musical never came to pass, although one did materialize in 1965—the ponderous *Baker Street*—in which, luckily, Wilder was not involved. Eventually Wilder would make a Holmes film, but it is doubtful that he could have captured the uniquely British flavor in Conan Doyle's stories, where reason and mystery become one in the sense that all mysteries have rational explanations, had he not conquered another British form—melodrama where the murder plot is as cunning as the means by which it is detected.

That Wilder was thinking of a Holmes scenario at the time he was working on the script of *Witness* is clear from a significant change he made in Christie's original to which he was generally faithful. Wilder added the character of Miss Plimsoll as a combination nurse-nanny-companion of a London barrister, Sir Wilfrid Robarts. With Charles Laughton as Sir Wilfrid and his wife, Elsa Lanchester, as Miss Plimsoll, the characters became an asexual couple like Holmes and Watson, each needing the other but unwilling to express anything so ordinary as affection. Sir Wilfrid rails at Miss Plimsoll, and she endures his insults because she idolizes him; he tolerates her nagging because he respects her. Just as Watson knew about Holmes's addiction to cocaine and his hiding place for his syringe, Miss Plimsoll knows that Sir Wilfrid fills his Thermos with brandy and pretends to be sipping cocoa in court.

Furthermore, the defendant's wife, Christine, affects a disguise that tricks Sir Wilfrid and leads to her husband's acquittal. Unlike Christie, Wilder emphasized the barrister's fascination with Christine, which was not very difficult with Marlene Dietrich playing the role. With Nurse Plimsoll as a female Dr. Watson, Christine Vole becomes an avatar of Irene Adler, the only woman who ever outwitted Sherlock Holmes.

Witness for the Prosecution (1958)

There is nothing about the opening of *Witness* to suggest a Billy Wilder film. The mood is more like a Twentieth Century–Fox movie of the 1940s, the kind that began with calligraphic credits and a stately overture. The credits for *Witness* appear as the Old Bailey, the chief criminal court of England, comes into session to the solemn measures of a Pomp and Circumstance-like march. It is significant that the first shot is of the Old Bailey. Since Leonard Vole's trial comprised so much of the action, Wilder made the court a character from the outset, giving it the dignity one expects venerable British institutions to have.

One also expects venerable British authors like Agatha Christie to be accorded similar respect. Although Wilder made changes in Christie's play, he did not revamp it as he did *Sabrina Fair*. However, he was faced with the task of filming a play in which one character tricks another and fools the audience as well. As is usually the case with Christie, the plot itself is quite simple; it is her art of misdirection that creates complexity.

Sir Wilfrid Robarts is asked to defend Leonard Vole, accused of murdering a wealthy widow. Vole's wife, known in the play as Romaine, learns that, according to British law, a wife cannot testify against her husband. When she appears in the witness box, she deliberately seems to be undermining her husband's alibi. Shortly afterwards, Sir Wilfrid receives a mysterious phone call from a

Billy Wilder on the set of *Witness for the Prosecution* with Charles Laughton and Marlene Dietrich.

woman claiming to have crucial evidence. When he and the woman meet, she sells him letters Romaine Vole wrote to her lover in which she expressed her desire to see her husband out of the way, so the two of them could be together. Sir Wilfrid produces the letters in court, thereby winning the case. Later, Romaine reveals that she was the mystery woman. Her disguise may have saved her husband, but not their marriage. Vole now has a new love interest, one considerably younger than Romaine. Rather than lose her husband to a rival, Romaine stabs him; and there is a very swift curtain.

Anyone familiar with the original probably expected Wilder to invent a new denouement. Ingeniously, Wilder retained Christie's denouement but devised, as we shall see, a new ending; thus, in the film, the resolution is distinct from the conclusion as opposed to the play where the resolution is the conclusion. Then there was the matter of opening up the play. Christie's play required only one other set besides the Old Bailey—the barrister's quarters. Naturally, Wilder added more scenes, but not as many as he did in *Sabrina*. His chief additions, apart from the brilliant conclusion and the character of Miss Plimsoll, were two flashbacks—one to show how Vole met the widow, and the other to show how he met his wife, now called Christine instead of Romaine. The sale of the letters takes place in a railway bar rather than in Sir Wilfrid's rooms. Generally, however, Wilder was as faithful to the original as a filmmaker can be to a two-set play.

In the movies, courtroom melodrama can be tedious because the action is confined to a physically circumscribed area with a minimum of movement and a maximum of dialogue. British courtroom procedure, in particular, could strike American audiences as wearisome because it is so ceremonious. Even Hitchcock was unable to inject much drama into the courtroom scenes in *The Paradine Case* (1948). However, the Old Bailey responded well to Wilder's sense of realism. As we have seen, realism to Wilder does not mean close-ups of gaping wounds or bodily parts. If anything, such attempts at realism provoke disgust or laughter because they separate the person from his body, reducing the person to a wound or an organ. What is disembodied is unreal; hence, the sight of it inspires revulsion or derision.

Realism is a respect for the real; it is a belief in the totality of experience, not in random moments. Film realism attempts to maintain the flow of existence by not blocking or diverting it through unnecessary cuts. Of course, a filmmaker must cut; but a realist will shoot a scene in such a way that the characters will be able to exchange some of the dialogue before the inevitable cuts from one to the other begin. For example, there is very little cutting in the scene when Vole protests his innocence. Vole is in the center of the frame; his solicitor, Mayhew, is in the background; right of frame is Sir Wilfrid, using his monocle to deflect the sunlight at Vole—a trick he employs for trapping liars. Vole blinks but is not unnerved.

When Marlene Dietrich makes her first appearance as Christine, Wilder does not cut to a close-up of the actress, as many directors would. Christine enters the action naturally, unobtrusively. At first, Sir Wilfrid refuses to take Vole's case because of his heart condition. As he ascends the stairs in a chair lift, he expresses his sympathy for Mrs. Vole, adding that she may need smelling salts when she hears the news. "I do not think that will be necessary," a voice replies. It is Christine's; but the audience hears her before it sees her.

It was a challenge to create tension in the courtroom scenes. In an American courtroom, a lawyer could pace up and down and peer into the jury's eyes; but the Old Bailey was not designed for such theatrics. Wilder had to film scenes where there was little or no movement. Thus he used as many long takes as possible, always cutting at the right moment. When Sir Wilfrid interrogates the police inspector, he is in the right of the frame and the inspector is in the witness box at the left. Wilder gets both men into the same shot; then he cuts from one to the other. Sometimes Wilder will reverse the procedure, as he did when Sir Wilfrid questioned the widow's deaf maid, Janet Mackenzie (Una O'Connor). Wilder cuts back and forth, from Sir Wilfrid to Janet, as he must in order to emphasize the character's deafness. As she is about to leave the witness box, Wilder frames the courtroom in long shot, with the departing Janet on the right and Sir Wilfrid on the left.

Film realism is also a matter of aligning the angle of vision with the appropriate shot. When Miss Plimsoll, seated in the gallery, beckons to Sir Wilfrid below, the shot has to be from a high angle— with the camera peering down on the courtroom. Likewise, when anyone in the courtroom looked up to the gallery, a low angle shot was required.

Wilder's sense of realism goes beyond long takes and angle shots; it extends to the very heart of the script and is reflected in the way he transforms Christie's stereotypes into people. Characterization was never Christie's strong point; it was up to the actors to put some human flesh on her skeletons. On Broadway Sir Wilfrid was played by Francis L. Sullivan. No less corpulent than Laughton, Sullivan wheezed through the role, creating a character out of nasal congestion and shortness of breath. Wilder turned Sir Wilfrid from a caricature into a character who was arbitrary, arrogant, and lovable—in short, into himself. By giving Sir Wilfrid a foil in Miss Plimsoll, Wilder humanized the character even further. When Sir Wilfrid and Miss Plimsoll are arguing in the opening scene—she chattering about his medication, he countering with insults that she ignores—Wilder immediately establishes Sir Wilfrid as a Restoration Scrooge who can toss off a line like "I'll snatch her thermometer and plunge it through her shoulder blades" as if it were one of Congreve's.

By the time he was cast as Leonard Vole, Tyrone Power had lost the Latin ardor he radiated in *The Mark of Zorro* (1940) and *Blood and Sand* (1941). He was now in that transitional stage between going to pot and going out to pasture; but he was still able to invest the part of Vole with a roguish deference toward women that would explain Christine's attraction to him. But does a rakish glint explain her willingness to perjure herself in order to win his acquittal? Why would a beautiful woman risk jail for a cad? In melodrama, the answer is simple—love; but it was not an answer that satisfied Wilder. What kind of love would inspire a woman to write a series of self-incriminating letters?

Wilder found the answer to that question in a seemingly insignificant point that is made about Christine in the play: she is German. Wilder used that fact as the basis of his characterization. Obviously, a mere reference to her German background will not be sufficient. Thus Wilder adds a flashback showing how Vole met his wife when she was singing in a cellar café in Hamburg shortly before the end of World War II. Everything about the scene conjures up other Dietrich characters: Lola-Lola in *The Blue Angel* (1930); Amy Jolly in *Morocco* (1930); and, of course, Erika in *A*

Foreign Affair. In fact, Christine's basement apartment is as much of a hovel as Erika's bombed-out flat in *A Foreign Affair.* Naturally, Christine feels grateful to Vole for bringing her to London, and her gratitude grows into love despite the fact that her husband detests work and fancies himself an inventor. Thus the transfigured look that appears on Christine's face when she hears the verdict is sincere; it is not just front lighting for Marlene Dietrich.

While Christine's scheme may not command total belief (what melodramatic ruse does?), she is still as credible as any other long-suffering heroine. As played by Dietrich, Christine has a mythic plausibility. Thus Wilder cannot desecrate a myth by sending Christine to the gallows, although she murders her husband in both the play and the film. Actually, it is in the very last scene that Wilder supplies the new ending that audiences were expecting; but he does it so subtly that some may think he simply filmed Christie's conclusion.

Wilder could no more sentence Christine to death for murdering a bounder than he could send Erika off to a labor camp without implying that she would never get there. But how does one justify murder, particularly one committed in the august Old Bailey? "She *executed* him," Sir Wilfrid notes. So it was not murder, but retribution; Christine was meting out the sentence that the jury would have if it had all the facts. "Remarkable woman," Sir Wilfrid muses. And one knows that the barrister will postpone his Bermuda vacation until he acquits Christine. Miss Plimsoll endorses his decision; brandishing the Thermos that supposedly contains cocoa, she calls after him, "You forgot your brandy!"—a closing line that is more humanly satisfying than the leaden rhetoric that ends the play. There Romaine says stoically, "I shall not be tried for perjury. I shall be tried for murder—the murder of the only man I ever loved." She then stabs her husband and adds, "Guilty, my lord." CURTAIN.

The Private Life of Sherlock Holmes (1970)

When Wilder was finally ready to make his Sherlock Holmes movie, there was already a considerable body of celluloid Holmesiana—notably the fourteen films made between 1939 and

1946 that featured Basil Rathbone as Holmes and Nigel Bruce as Watson. Wilder needed a fresh approach—not reworked Conan Doyle or pseudo–Conan Doyle, but neo–Conan Doyle; new adventures in the old tradition. Wilder begins *The Private Life of Sherlock Holmes* by fading in on a brass plaque outside a London bank; its polished surface reflects those red double-decker buses that roam around London. We do not have to be reminded we are in present-day London; the camera has informed us with an unobtrusive time-place designation. An elegant credits sequence follows with voice-over narration; it is Watson's voice, addressing his heirs. He reminds them that, in the vault of a London bank, there is a dispatch box waiting to be opened. Watson's will had stipulated that the box could not be opened until fifty years after his death; the fifty years are now up. The credits continue as the contents of the box are carefully removed. It is mostly memorabilia—a magnifying glass, a stethoscope, a hypodermic needle, and, finally, stories that were withheld from the public because of their "delicate and sometimes scandalous nature."

The dusty manuscript is both Wilder's invention and his innovation; the film, then, becomes the dramatization of these previously unpublished stories. But the key is the plangent violin music of the credits sequence; music perhaps as bittersweet as the kind Holmes played to console himself. Miklós Rózsa, whose Violin Concerto was used as background music for the film, distilled the essence of sadness into a score of such purity that it conveys loss in its most naked, abstract form. Holmes's new adventures, then, will not be the usual sleuthing around in foggy, gaslit London; they will portray a born romantic whose pursuit of the rational made him reason's slave and allowed him only two forms of relaxation—the violin and the hypodermic.

Wilder is demythologizing Holmes. At the beginning of the film, Holmes accuses Watson of creating a superhuman, six-foot sleuth in a deerstalker and cape who was a violin virtuoso, a misogynist, and a dope addict. In a sense, this is also Wilder accusing Hollywood of perpetuating a similar myth and never proceeding from the myth to the man. Why would a man who cultivated reason find solace in cocaine except to compensate for a life devoid of love? At the end of Conan Doyle's *The Sign of the Four*, Watson says, "You have done all the work in this business. I get a wife out of it . . . pray what remains for you?" Holmes answers immediately, "For me, there still remains the cocaine-bottle."[1] It is as if the mere mention of "wife" sent Holmes's "long white hand" reaching up for his substitute.

The Holmes portrayed in the version of the film that was released in the fall of 1970 was not quite as demythologized as Wilder had planned. The original script called for four adventures. Wilder had intended to explain Holmes's so-called misogyny by depicting a student love affair between Holmes and a girl who was really a prostitute.[2] According to Miklós Rózsa, the film was supposed to open with a train sequence in which Holmes, on the basis of a pair of shoes and a tuning fork, deduces that the man in his compartment is a Neapolitan music teacher who has just had a narrow escape from a lady's boudoir because he is wearing the slippers of her husband, the Duke of Naples.[3] There was also to have been a cruise ship murder with arsenic-laced champagne. Another deleted episode was "The Upside Down Room" in which Watson and Inspector Lestrade, to alleviate Holmes's boredom and distract him from his cocaine, concocted a case for him involving a room where everything was topsy-turvy.

All of these adventures—both those in the original version of the film that ran over three hours and those in the two-hour film that United Artists released in 1970—were original. They seem to be authentic, however, because Wilder used motifs from Conan Doyle's stories as points of departure for the cases he invented for Holmes and Watson. For example, in the film, Holmes conducts elaborate experiments with tobacco as a source of clues as well as criminal traits. In both *The Sign of the Four* and "The Boscombe Valley Mystery," Holmes alludes to his monograph in which he isolated 140 varieties of pipe, cigar, and cigarette tobacco. The Loch Ness adventure, which revolves around Britain's attempt to perfect a submarine, does not appear in an actual Conan Doyle story. However, the theft of submarine plans occurs in "The Adventure of the Bruce-Partington Plans." In "The Adventure of the Engineer's Thumb," an engineer is tricked into checking a hydraulic press which is secretly being used for minting fake coins by a counterfeit ring that includes a sinister German; in the film, a Belgian engineer is hired to perfect an air pump for the submarine the British are trying to develop before German agents, disguised as Trappist monks, steal the plans.

In the Loch Ness adventure, Wilder shows his familiarity with the Conan Doyle biography. Conan Doyle was quite knowledgeable about submarines, as he revealed in his 1912 story "Danger!" However, before World War I, Conan Doyle spoke out on Britain's need to build up a submarine fleet as protection against the German U-boats.[4] In the film Queen Victoria refuses to use the submarine as a warship; she prefers that it be used to study marine life—an ironic gloss on Britain's unpreparedness for submarine warfare at the outbreak of World War I. It is touches such as these that make *The Private Life of Sherlock Holmes* such a perfect recreation of Conan Doyle's world.

That Wilder could achieve such a successful recreation is even more amazing when one considers that he had to cut over an hour from the original version; yet, even though he reduced the four adventures to two, he did not alter the film's unity. Only someone able to cope with the vagaries of script surgery—where a movie is altered, amputated, or restored as a result of slashed budgets; locations that prove unsatisfactory; stars who must be replaced; or, in the present case, a studio that was dissatisfied—can excise without mutilating. What unites the two adventures in *The Private Life of Sherlock Holmes* seems totally unrelated: a newspaper account of the disappearance of some midgets who were part of an acrobatic act, and the plot of Tchaikovsky's ballet, *Swan Lake*.

Holmes receives a pair of tickets in the mail for a performance of *Swan Lake*; they are the gift of a Russian ballerina who wants Holmes to impregnate her so the world can be graced with a child of genius and beauty. Holmes declines; but, rather than offend the lady, he alleges that he and Watson are lovers. Of course, Holmes is lying; but later, when he and Watson are backstage, the news of their relationship travels around the company. One by one, eager but effete-looking male dancers replace the ballerinas who were kicking up their heels with Watson.

Although the story Holmes fabricates about himself and Watson seems designed to get an easy laugh, Wilder is not playing the imp as he sometimes does. He uses the tale to introduce the film's most important theme: Holmes's quest for the ideal woman, or, in Jungian terms, for the *anima*—the feminine principle that is both the source and the archetype of life. The *anima* has two faces—the malefic one, seen in the crones and witches of fairy tales; and the benign one belonging to the princesses and blessed damsels. Both types of women appear in the film. There is something witchlike about the ballerina, with her raven-black hair and her chalk-white face that looks drained of blood. Naturally, Holmes rejects her; but his tragedy is that he will also never be able to possess the princess when she enters his life.

The critics who have been cataloguing homosexual motifs in Wilder's films welcomed *The Private Life of Sherlock Holmes*.[5] At the risk of undermining their scholarship, one must insist upon a distinction between homosexual and homoerotic. Whenever men live together—in an apartment, a barracks, a boarding school, a prison compound—a homoerotic atmosphere is inevitable. The men will begin to take on characteristics ordinarily associated with heterosexual married couples: they will divide responsibilities, display affection, express feelings of rejection, grow sullen, or lapse into silences that belie their mutual devotion. Wilder, as we have seen, laid the groundwork for the Holmes-Watson friendship in *Witness for the Prosecution*, where Miss Plimsoll played nagging wife to Sir Wilfrid's testy husband; similarly, Watson scolds Holmes for taking cocaine. In fact, Watson becomes so disgusted with Holmes's refusal to give up the habit that he threatens to leave 221B Baker Street and acts like a wife at her wits' end. Holmes placates Watson by firing his revolver at the cocaine bottles, hiding the real ones in his violin case.

Wilder leaves no doubt that Holmes and Watson are men, not homosexuals in disguise or even homosexuals in the flesh. They may no longer be enjoying the heyday in the blood (although Watson still boasts of his prowess), but that does not make them another Oscar Wilde and Lord Alfred Douglas. Thus Watson is rightly annoyed when he learns of the story Holmes told the ballerina; inevitably, his annoyance leads to a discussion of women. Watson plays the outraged Don Juan, boasting that he can get women from three continents to testify to his manhood. "And you can get women to vouch for you, too, can't you, Holmes?" he asks. Holmes does not reply. Anxiously, Watson repeats the question as if their friendship depended on an affirmative reply. "The answer is 'yes,'" Holmes responds icily and shuts his bedroom door. Holmes's answer is an amalgam of pique and forthrightness; he is irritated that sex should even enter the conversation, but at the same time realizes that a friend's question deserves an answer. Perhaps the deleted scene with the prostitute might have cast some light on Holmes's earlier remark: "I don't dislike women; I merely distrust them." But Robert Stephens, who plays Holmes superbly, delivered the line, "The answer is 'yes,'" with such agonizing honesty that one knew it was spoken by a man who was not ignorant of heartbreak.

The conversation about women leads to the second adventure, which also involves a woman. The link is voice-over; one must remember that the film is a dramatization of Watson's stories written, as usual, in the first person. Watson's voice, then, will be heard intermittently, as happens now: "What, indeed, was his attitude toward women? Was there some secret he was holding back? Or was he just a thinking machine, incapable of any emotion?"

The question is answered in the second adventure, which begins as a cabbie deposits a woman on Holmes's doorstep. She is wet and dazed; her name appears to be Gabrielle Valladon (Genevieve Page). That night, she sleepwalks in the nude, mistaking Holmes for her husband, Emile. In the sleepwalking scene, Wilder achieves something quite unusual—a chaste eroticism as Gabrielle extends her arms toward Holmes, who looks at her with an expression of detachment and fascination.

Wilder continues this mood of decorous sensuality in the train sequence when Holmes and Gabrielle, using the names of Mr. and Mrs. Ashdown, travel to Inverness, where they hope to locate Emile Valladon. In the sleeper, Gabrielle takes the lower berth; Holmes, the upper. They reverse the order of berths in *The Major and the Minor*, where Susan occupied the upper and Kirby the lower. In the intervening years, Wilder learned a great deal about visual eroticism. As Holmes and Gabrielle playfully bid each other goodnight under their assumed names, the camera tilts down from Holmes to Gabrielle. As she slips off to sleep, her face radiates fulfillment; one would almost believe she was Mrs. Sherlock Holmes.

Once they arrive at Inverness, Wilder moves from romance to pure adventure. Ultimately, they find Valladon, but not until they encounter a succession of mysteries. What appears to be the Loch Ness monster causes their boat to capsize. They watch some midgets being buried, but one of the coffins is far too large for a midget. When the coffin is opened, it contains three white canaries and Emile Valladon's body; equally mysterious is the fact that Valladon's wedding ring has turned green. Suddenly there is the flash of recognition; it is the scenario of *Swan Lake*, as Holmes explains to Watson: "There is a lake, and there's a castle; and there's a swan that really isn't a swan; or, in this case, a monster that isn't really a monster."

Wilder has come up with a dazzlingly rational explanation for these strange events, confirming what Holmes said in "The Adventure of the Noble Bachelor" about some of his own bizarre cases—namely, that there is always a simple explanation for the inexplicable. Emile Valladon was hired by a fictitious firm called Jonah Ltd., a front for the British Foreign Office, to perfect an air pump for a submarine the British were secretly testing at Inverness. The periscope was camouflaged with a gargoyle to resemble the legendary monster of Loch Ness. The submarine was manned by a team of midgets—the same ones that had disappeared earlier; it was operated by sulphuric acid batteries with canaries used to detect chlorine gas. Apparently, Valladon was asphyxiated when a leak in the hull caused sea water to mix with the acid, producing chlorine gas that turned his ring green and the canaries white.

Holmes was right about *Swan Lake*; it was a metaphor for the Inverness adventure. However, there is another feature of the ballet that also applies to Holmes—deception by a woman. In *Swan Lake*, the villain Rotbart tricks Prince Siegfried by spiriting away the beautiful Odette and substituting his daughter, the wicked Odile, in her place. Just as Odile was not Odette, although she looked exactly like her, Holmes's traveling companion is not Gabrielle Valladon; she is Ilse von Hoffmanstahl, a German spy. Ilse's model is, of course, Irene Adler, whom Holmes always called "*the woman*," as Watson tells us at the end of "A Scandal in Bohemia." Like Irene, Ilse outwits the master sleuth, the only woman ever to do so.

When Holmes must confront Ilse with the fact that he knows who she is, Stephens and Page play the scene with the right undercurrent of civilized regret; these are two proud people who obviously admire each other, trying to express their mutual admiration by what they leave unsaid. In a shot epitomizing feminine grace, Ilse draws the veil of her hat over her face and leaves, presumably to be exchanged for a British prisoner. As her carriage proceeds up the path, she flashes Holmes a message in code with her parasol: "Auf Wiedersehen."

But it was not to be. At the end of the film, Holmes learns that Ilse was executed as a spy in Japan, where she worked under the name of Mrs. Ashdown. Immediately, one hears Rózsa's violin motif; the tension of tears suppressed and feelings denied vibrates in the strings, which seem about to snap. "Where is it, Watson?" Holmes asks. Finding his cocaine, Holmes retires to his room. Again, one cannot help but think of Holmes's final words in *The Sign of the Four*: "For me, there still remains the cocaine-bottle."

With the first network telecast of *The Private Life of Sherlock Holmes* in the summer of 1978, and the ever-increasing number of revivals it has been receiving, the film now occupies a prominent place in the Wilder canon. If United Artists ever releases the original version (apparently, a print exists in London), one hopes it will have the homogeneity of the cut version. From what one has read about the deleted episodes, less may be more. As it is, Wilder has never defined a society as accurately as he did in *Holmes*. One of the main conflicts of the Victorian age—the excitement of science which bound man to the present versus the desire for beauty that sent him back to the past—pervades the film. To Wilder's Holmes, reason was an activity of the present; mystery, the pursuit of the past. Holmes may never have been able to reconcile reason and emotion within himself; but he was able to reconcile reason and mystery in his cases. That the two could be made compatible is not difficult to understand; every mystery has a rational explanation. Holmes's ability to practice the twin arts of deduction and reconciliation kept him from developing into a psychically cleft Dorian Gray or a Henry Jekyll.

On the one hand, Wilder has been faithful to the Holmes portrait in Conan Doyle's *A Study in Scarlet*, where the detective has such a "turn both for observation and deduction" that he knows immediately that Watson has just come from Afghanistan; on the other, Wilder has been faithful to himself. He had no intention of making a movie about Holmes the thinking machine, but about Holmes the man. But because Wilder's Holmes does not sob into the lens or raise his fist to heaven, one may think he is not human. Yet there can be as much emotion in the way a man looks longingly but chastely at a naked woman, or in the way two intelligent people say goodbye without becoming maudlin, as there is in Lawrentian sex or grand opera. Holmes's emotions are civilized; he lives the amenities the way most people live life. Holmes has something Billy Wilder has often been accused of lacking—taste.

12

Down among the Rotting Palms: *Sunset Boulevard* and *Fedora*

The Price of Hollywood

THE NAME OF HOLLYWOOD has rarely denoted anything positive. Hollywood is the dream factory, tinseltown, lotusland. A studio head is a mogul; a studio lot, a dream dump. A Hollywood ending is one in which a situation that cannot possibly end happily does. A Hollywood mentality believes stars never get pimples or move their bowels. A Hollywood column is run on gossip *à la* Hedda Hopper, Louella Parsons, Rona Barrett, or Rex Reed. A Broadway star has talent; a Hollywood star has a synthetic personality created by a studio or a press agent.

The movie star performs not before a live audience but before a dead one—the fastidious but inanimate camera. Movie acting is the art of pleasing the inanimate; it is the technique of discovering which side of the face the camera favors of what type or lighting accentuates the cheekbones or straightens the nose. The very mention of the word "camera" excites a star. In *Sunset Boulevard*, it is only when Norma Desmond hears there are cameras downstairs that she agrees to leave her boudoir and greet them, descending the staircase like a deranged bride. "There's nothing else; just us and the camera," she whispers to her imaginary colleagues.

It is not surprising that death and Hollywood have much in common; to Nathanael West in *The Day of the Locust*, it was an Eden of death. Hollywood conjures up images of stars' footprints in cement; tourists gazing reverentially at the vault in Forest Lawn that contains Betty Grable's ashes; and maps to the burial places of the stars that are as popular as the maps to the stars' homes.

Moviemaking is a variation on the death-rebirth cycle. A

149

The Price of Hollywood: Bandaged wrists and dark glasses.
(Top) Gloria Swanson and William Holden in Sunset Boulevard; *(bottom) Marthe Keller and William Holden in* Fedora.

reflection in a mirror is a dead image; so is a star's when it is transferred to celluloid. Moviemaking is the transformation of living beings into dead images which are then given life by being projected on a screen. Moviegoing is watching dead images coming out of a projector ordinarily at the rate of twenty-four frames per second. Since the stars have "died" by giving up their image to celluloid, they can be immortal both in their lifetime and after their death. Humphrey Bogart, Judy Garland, and Marilyn Monroe are as alive as they ever were. New generations keep discovering them, responding to them as one responds to the living, referring to them intimately if their screen personae allowed familiarity (Bogie, Judy, Monty, Elvis) or by their last name if they exuded aloofness or mystery (Gable, Tracy, Crawford). Movies, then, are the ultimate death-in-life; or, as Ginger Rogers summed it up after a retrospective, "I'm me"—making a distinction between her living self and her celluloid equivalent.

Therefore, the most truthful movie about Hollywood would be one that would dramatize the paradox that a star dies to the camera and is reborn from it. Until *Sunset Boulevard*, there were two basic types of movies about Hollywood: the grim and the giddy. One either witnessed the rise and fall of a star—e.g., *Show People* (1929), *What Price Hollywood?* (1932); *A Star Is Born* (1937); or one just witnessed the rise from obscurity to fame—e.g., *The Goldwyn Follies* (1938); *Variety Girl* (1947). Stars either hit the bottle like Norman Maine in *A Star Is Born*, or they came to the aid of an unknown, the way Paramount's contract players did in *Variety Girl*, to turn Mary Thatcher into one of their own. Life at the studio was either strictly business (*Hold Back the Dawn*, 1941); or strictly mayhem (*Never Give a Sucker an Even Break*, 1941).

Yet none of these films faced the unassailable fact that moviemaking is necromancy; it is literally bringing the dead to life. *Sunset Boulevard* did; the reversible death-rebirth cycle constituted the film's theme and image pattern.[1] For Wilder, it was not enough simply to make a movie about moviemaking, as Preston Sturges had done in *Sullivan's Travels* (1941). Although Wilder makes Paramount an important part of *Sunset Boulevard* and sets a certain number of scenes at the studio, he is not working in the tradition of the movie movie. He is pushing film necromancy to its limit by making Norma Desmond, his heroine, a silent star who decides to return to the screen when the sound era is almost a quarter of a century old; and, even more tragically, at a time when the movies are yielding to television as the mass medium.

As if that were not enough, Wilder insisted Norma be played by an actress who had herself experienced an eclipse; a former movie queen who was now in the "whatever became of" category. First Wilder approached Mae West, whose own film career was sporadic; at that time her latest movie was *The Heat's On* (1943). Mae was insulted. Next he sounded out Mary Pickford, who had not worked in films since 1933; "America's Sweetheart" wanted more control over the script than Wilder was willing to give her. Then he tried Pola Negri, whose own career bore a sad resemblance to Norma's. Although Negri made some sound films, she never really managed the transition from the silents to the talkies. She also bristled at the prospect of playing a has-been. Finally George Cukor suggested Gloria Swanson, who agreed with one stipulation: she would not do a screen test.

Wilder understood actresses who possessed what Jung would call a "numinous" personality, one that was so dazzlingly mythic that it evoked the goddesses of antiquity. Wilder kept their mythology intact, but he also tailored the character to fit the mythology. In so doing, he exposed, ever so subtly, the star's real—as opposed to mythic—center. In *A Foreign Affair*, he created a Dietrich icon whose face, tightened into a mask of immobility, proclaimed the character's right to live by her own moral code—as Marlene Dietrich herself has always done. In his two films with Marilyn Monroe, he released the love child within the love goddess, the potentially self-destructive waif within the flesh queen. In a sense, Marilyn's performance in *Some Like It Hot* was a preview of her grand exit three years later.

Similarly, Wilder made Gloria Swanson the prototypical silent star so obsessed with glamour that she was chauffeured in an Isotta-Fraschini upholstered in leopard skin. There was even a similarity in the names of Gloria Swanson and Norma Desmond. Actually, there was no Gloria Swanson; there was only a Josephine Swenson who became Gloria Swanson. Josephine Swenson was rechristened with the Hollywood dream name—nonsectarian, aristocratic, and mythic. Inevitably, moviegoers would connect Gloria Swanson with Norma Desmond. Their names—the ultimate in Hollywood nomenclature—are not only similar in cadence, but they are names that leave behind a mental picture of those who bear them. Thus one imagines a *grande dame*, watching her old movies in a living room crammed with memorabilia. Swanson, of course, was never a recluse; but Wilder pushed her mythology to the extreme where decadence is the underside of glamour; and madness, the price of nostalgia.

There was no malevolence in what Wilder did, although some have suggested there was.[2] Wilder could respect a star's mythology and, at the same time, expose the roots of that mythology; the source that manufactures the mask to cover what nature left incomplete. On the one hand, there is the iconic Swanson—the epitome of 1920s chic; on the other, there is an actress with a voice that is weak and childlike—a defect she shares with many silent stars. Wilder used both the myth and the reality underlying it to create the character of Norma Desmond. For what today we would call a silent star's failings (exaggerated gestures, operatic mannerisms) were really part of the star's mythology.

This is how Wilder operates. If a star reveals something of himself or herself in the character—as all of Wilder's stars, including the males, have done—it is because Wilder saw something of the star in the character to begin with. And the rest is myth-making.

Sunset Boulevard (1950)

The film does not open like a storybook, the way the 1937 *A Star Is Born* did. *Sunset Boulevard* actually opens in the gutter, with leaves swirling in a crazy circle. The title is painted on the curb. A tracking shot takes the viewer up the boulevard as the credits appear in the same wedge-shaped letters. It might be more accurate to say that the camera does a mad tango up the boulevard to Franz Waxman's frenetic score that sounds like Strauss's "Dance of the Seven Veils" from *Salome* reorchestrated to resemble Ravel's *Bolero*. When the credits end, a voice is heard saying, "Yes, this is Sunset Boulevard; Los Angeles, California."

The voice belongs to a dead man floating, face downward, in a pool; it is the voice of screenwriter, Joe Gillis (William Holden). The film, then, will be a flashback with voice-over narration. Since

Double Indemnity, Wilder has used voice-over either as a kind of prologue (*The Apartment; One, Two, Three*) or as a way of bridging the flashbacks (*The Emperor Waltz, Stalag 17, Fedora*). However, Cookie, the narrator of *Stalag 17,* was alive; so was the dowager of *The Emperor Waltz* who was telling her cronies about Virgil and Johanna. Joe Gillis, on the other hand, is dead.

Narration by a corpse is unusual in any medium, although it was attempted in a Bela Lugosi movie that has become a cult favorite, *Scared to Death* (1947). Certainly, such a type of narration would seem to break the laws of verisimilitude; but it works perfectly in *Sunset Boulevard,* which is a film about the living dead, told by one who, for a time, was part of their circle. But Gillis is not a typical corpse; he is a corpse who wants reportorial accuracy. Thus he will tell his story before the press has a chance to distort it. Already Wilder was rehearsing for his next film, *The Big Carnival,* which would portray such distortion.

Gillis is a combination hustler–con artist, neither endearing nor smarmy, but just inoffensively opportunistic. There are, as usual, certain affinities between Wilder and his character. As a Los Angeleno, Gillis needs his car, but his creditors are after it. Wilder also had difficulty keeping up payments on his 1928 De Soto in the mid 1930s. Gillis is a struggling screenwriter, peddling a script called *Bases Loaded;* Wilder also knew the frustration of hawking scripts.

Although Gillis suggests the Wilder of the lean years (1934–37), there is nothing of the 1930s in *Sunset Boulevard.* In fact, the film was uncommonly contemporary. Wilder made it in the spring of 1949, the year in which the film is set. The script is filled with references to the 1940s. Gillis envisions *Bases Loaded* as a vehicle for Alan Ladd with a featured part for character actor William Demarest, both of whom were contract players at Paramount then. Sheldrake (Wilder's favorite surname), the studio head, recommends that Gillis rewrite the script for Betty Hutton and make her the star player of a girls' softball team. At an assistant director's New Year's Eve party, the guests, largely Paramount employees, sing their own version of "Buttons and Bows," the hit song of the Bob Hope–Jane Russell comedy *The Paleface* (1948).

This is the now Hollywood without Vaseline on the lens to give it an otherworldly glow. Even the "meet cute" is perverse: Norma mistakes Gillis for an undertaker and ushers him into the bedroom, where he sees a simian arm hanging out of a coffin; it belongs to Norma's dead monkey. When Norma discovers Gillis is a screenwriter, she keeps him on to help her revise the script she has written for her comeback—the story of Salome in which she, a woman of at least fifty, would play the biblical princess. Gillis, needing money as well as a place to hide from his creditors, agrees; he also becomes her kept man. At the same time, he is seeing Betty Schaefer (Nancy Olson), a young story editor at Paramount, who believes one of his scripts has promise. Yet Gillis does not leave Norma for Betty; he leaves Norma because he is tired of being a successful gigolo but a failed writer. But, to quote Norma, "Nobody leaves a star." As Gillis walks out of the mansion, Norma shoots him; staggering across the patio, he falls into the pool.

"Cruel" is an adjective often associated with *Sunset Boulevard*. Some have thought it "cruel" of Wilder to cast Erich von Stroheim as Max von Mayerling, Norma's butler and former husband. First, the names are soundalikes. Also, Max was once a major director; so was von Stroheim, whose directorial career also ended with the silents. As an actor, von Stroheim went from the classic *Grand Illusion* (1937) to potboilers at Republic such as *The Lady and the Monster* (1944) and *The Great Flammarion* (1945). Yet von Stroheim brought a quality to the role that only someone who had experienced the vicissitudes of fortune could—humility. But it was not a humility purchased at the expense of dignity. Max is still the aristocrat, even when he answers the door or pours champagne at Norma's spectral New Year's Eve party. Ironically Max does get a chance to direct again; he stands in front of the newsreel cameras, pretending to be Cecil B. De Mille as Norma begins her mad descent down the stairs. Von Stroheim was not quite so lucky; his only sound film, *Walking Down Broadway* (1933), was reedited and released as *Hello, Sister!* Again Wilder worked the persona into the character and the reality into the myth. Just as von Stroheim was willing to accept roles in B movies, Max also did not think it was beneath his dignity to take second billing to Norma, who was once his protégée and later his wife.

If this is cruelty, then it is cruelty designed to elicit compassion. Before one can be sympathetic to characters like Max and Norma, one must first see them exposed and vulnerable. There are few moments in film as brutally honest, or as poignant, as the one in which Norma suddenly stands up during a screening of one of her movies and swears, "I'll be up there again, so help me!" As she makes her vow, a cone of light from the projector turns her face a sickly silver.

It is an eerie kind of pathos that Wilder generates for Norma; it is similar to the pity one feels for Lucia during the mad scene in Donizetti's *Lucia di Lammermoor* when she descends the staircase in a state of sweet delirium—the flute imitating the ethereal sounds she must be hearing. There is something equally touching yet bizarre about the scene where Norma is on a Paramount sound-stage, waiting for De Mille to finish shooting. A microphone, suspended on the end of a boom, passes over her head and brushes against the feather of her hat. Norma treats the boom mike as if it were a fly—dismissing it with an impatient wave of the hand as, indeed, she dismissed sound from the movies. Then Norma hears a voice from the catwalk; it is a lighting man who remembers her from the old days at Paramount. He throws a spot on her; in a touching high shot, Norma is spotlit as a star should be. Word passes among the extras that Norma Desmond is on the set; suddenly she is thronged by old admirers, some of whom are even older than she. Wilder uses another high shot at Norma's New Year's Eve party that consists of herself, Gillis, an orchestra that plays "Diane" over and over, and Max as bartender. As Norma and Gillis dance, the only couple on an empty floor, Wilder cuts to a high shot to convey a feeling of ghostly desolation.

While one can be compassionate toward Norma, Wilder does not make it easy to like her any more than Tennessee Williams made it easy to like Blanche in *A Streetcar Named Desire*. One may commiserate with Norma and Blanche; one may even weep over their descents into madness. But both of them have traits—Norma's narcissism and overbearing manner, Blanche's airs and neurotic flightiness—that are grating. However, part of Wilder's genius is his ability to create ambivalent characters, probably because he was ambivalent about them himself. When Norma extols the "purity" of the silents ("We didn't need dialogue; we had faces"), one hears, as if in an echo chamber, the wearisome argument that the movies died with sound; one also thinks of an earlier generation that had to listen to hoary English professors

using 1616, the year of Shakespeare's death, to mark the end of the
drama. Wilder is by no means advocating a return to the silents.
Although he began his career writing scripts for silent films in
Germany, he could never have become the kind of director he did
without words—a form of communication that Norma finds
anathema: "They opened their mouths, and what came out?
Words, words, more words!"

Norma is obviously not Wilder's mouthpiece. In fact, Wilder has
Gillis say at one point, "Audiences don't know somebody writes a
picture. They think the actors make it up as they go along." In the
film, Wilder tries to show how difficult screenwriting is. Gillis's
sessions with Norma on the *Salome* script must have been similar
to the ones Wilder had with Brackett as they argued over lines,
transposed, cut, and revised.

Visually *Sunset Boulevard* alternates between images of rotting
sumptuousness and sumptuous rot. Rats scamper about in an
unfilled swimming pool with weeds growing out of the cracks; a
tennis net sags over a court with faded markings; a pet monkey is
buried ceremoniously in a satin-lined coffin in Norma's garden; air
wheezes through the organ in Norma's living room. Norma sleeps
in a bed built in the shape of a ship, although it really looks like an
oversized cradle. Her parlor is filled with so many mementos of
her past that pictures of Norma Desmond crowd each other off the
tables.

Some of Wilder's shots have the impact of dramatic foreshadow-
ing. When Max explains to Gillis that Norma's frequent suicide
attempts have necessitated the removal of all the locks from the
doors, Wilder swish pans from one lockless door to another. Wilder
has always known when to use words and when an image will
suffice. After the abortive New Year's Eve party, Norma rushes up
the stairs past a mirror that fleetingly captures her reflection. The
camera moves in for a close-up of the bedroom door where the
lock has been removed. What will happen is inevitable.

The world of *Sunset Boulevard* is one of surfeit and isolation.
Thus some of Wilder's compositions are intentionally massive and
bigger than life. After the suicide attempt, Norma's bandaged
wrist, left of frame, greets Gillis like a grim artifact when he comes
through the bedroom door. When Gillis walks into the parlor, Max
is playing the organ; his hands seem to project into the frame as

"All right, Mr. De Mille. I'm ready for my close up." –The legendary Norma Desmond in *Sunset Boulevard*. (Erich von Stroheim looks on.)

Credit: Movie Star News

they crash upon the keys. But it is also a world that is so insular it is claustrophobic. A salesman, knowing that Norma is paying for Gillis's new wardrobe, tries to interest him in a vicuña coat. Wilder frames both men in a stifling two-shot, the salesman giving a knowing glance to Gillis, who returns it with a look of disgust.

Norma's plan for a comeback was mad, and the only way she will ever face the cameras will be in a state of madness. Wilder has staged a finale of operatic grandeur for her. To the sinuous rhythms of Franz Waxman's score, Norma makes a serpentine descent down the staircase, her arms raised for the dance she will never perform. She has improvised a Salome costume; her eyelids glitter with stardust, and rhinestones nestle in her hair. Oblivious to everything, she confuses her living room with a soundstage, newsreel cameras with movie cameras, the reporters with the *Salome* cast, and Max with Cecil B. De Mille. "All right, Mr. De Mille; I'm ready for my close-up," Norma says as she walks right into the lens without blinking at the light that floods her face.

Sunset Boulevard was a film of terminations. It marked the end of Hollywood's golden age, the end of stars like Norma Desmond, and the end of the "happiest couple in Hollywood." After twelve years together and thirteen pictures, Brackett and Wilder went their separate ways. Various reasons were given for the breakup. Paramount claimed their combined salary of $400,000 was too costly; the studio thought it could get more out of each of them— ideally, a film a year—if the team were dissolved. Another story was that Brackett's contempt for Sam Briskin, head of production, led to his leaving Paramount. Then there is Garson Kanin's version: Wilder simply told Brackett it would be better if they no longer worked together; and that was that.[3]

Brackett went to Twentieth Century–Fox, where he produced and collaborated on the screenplays of such films as *The Model and the Marriage Broker* (1951), *Titanic* (1953), *Teenage Rebel* (1956), and *Journey to the Center of the Earth* (1959). After the failure of *Cleopatra* (1962), one of Fox's costliest films, two thousand employees were fired in a single day; one of them was Charles Brackett, who had two more years to go on his contract. Wilder protested Fox's treatment of Brackett, but it was futile. Brackett died seven years later, in 1969.

Wilder did not find another permanent collaborator until he teamed up with I. A. L. Diamond for *Love in the Afternoon* (1957). Except for *Witness for the Prosecution,* "Iz" Diamond has collaborated on the script of every film he has directed since *Love in the Afternoon*—thus far, eleven films. Like Wilder, Diamond was an immigrant. Born in Rumania, Diamond came to the United States at the age of nine. He was educated at Boys High School in Brooklyn and then went to Columbia University, where he was editor of *The Spectator.* He also wrote sketches and lyrics for Columbia's varsity shows. His talent for comedy writing brought him an offer from Paramount, where he went after graduating from Columbia in 1941. Diamond languished at Paramount for eighteen months and then decided to freelance. His first film credit was Universal's horror-comedy *Murder in the Blue Room* (1944). He also collaborated on scripts at Warner Bros.—e.g., *Love and Learn* (1946), *Two Guys from Texas* (1948), *The Girl from Jones Beach* (1949). In the early 1950s he went over to Twentieth Century–Fox, where he worked on the scripts of *Love Nest* (1951), *Monkey Business* (1952), and *Something for the Birds* (1952).

Diamond's forte was comedy; even when he worked apart from Wilder on the Danny Kaye film *Merry Andrew* (1958) and *Cactus Flower* (1969), he was still on familiar ground. Perhaps it is significant that, with Diamond, Wilder made his greatest comedies—*Some Like It Hot* and *The Apartment*. But he could never make a *Sunset Boulevard* with Diamond; he could, however, make *Fedora* (1978).

Billy Wilder as Norma Desmond

If the history of *Fedora* sounds like the combined careers of Billy Wilder and Norma Desmond, it is not coincidental.[4] Sometimes art imitates life with a vengeance. As De Mille said ruefully about Norma in *Sunset Boulevard*, "Thirty million fans have given her the brush." A quarter of a century later, after not having had a smash hit since *Irma La Douce*, Wilder could say the same of himself.

In September 1973, Universal offered Wilder the chance to work at a studio again; he was to collaborate on the screenplay of *The Front Page* and direct the film for Universal. His office would be Lucille Ball's old dressing room; his neighbors, Alfred Hitchcock and Edith Head. In the 1940s, Wilder hardly thought he would ever be at Universal in the role of "visiting professor," as he termed his brief stay (September 1973–April 1977) at the studio.[5] Then, Universal was known for horror films, Abbott and Costello comedies, and desert camp with Maria Montez and Jon Hall. However, in the early 1970s, Universal, now a subsidiary of MCA (Music Corporation of America), was responsible for such commercial successes as *Airport* (1970), *American Graffiti* (1973), and *The Sting* (1973). *The Front Page* made a modest profit, and in 1976, Universal announced that Wilder would coauthor, produce, and direct *Fedora*, the first of four novellas in Thomas Tryon's *Crowned Heads*.

Knowing what it is like to be a dinosaur in a world of sleek and graceful mammals, Wilder felt he was ready to make a statement about Hollywood. And he felt he could make it within the context of *Fedora*, whose eponymous heroine was a legendary movie queen who never seemed to age. Her method of self-perpetuation was quite simple: she passed her daughter off as herself.

Fedora posed enormous problems for Wilder. Ideally, mother and daughter should be played by the same actress, and it could have been done. George Arliss played both father and son in *House of Rothschild* (1934). In Wilder's own *The Major and the Minor*, Ginger Rogers played Susan Applegate, a career woman in her late twenties; the twelve-year-old Sue-Sue; and Susan's mother, a woman in her mid-fifties. In *Payment on Demand* (1951), Bette Davis played a woman in middle age; and, in a flashback, the same woman as a young bride. But these were stars of the past. In 1976, there was no actress with anything even resembling a screen mythology who could play both Fedora and her daughter. There was no shortage of talented actresses; but none of them could evoke Hollywood's golden age, as Fedora must.

Wilder first thought of Marlene Dietrich and Faye Dunaway as a mother-daughter combination; but Dietrich, like Pola Negri and Mae West before her, despised the idea. Utlimately, Wilder ended up with two fine actresses—Hildegard Knef as Fedora and Marthe Keller as her daughter, called Antonia in the film; but neither had the iconic power to conjure up memories of the stars of yesteryear. Thus one is almost forced to take *Fedora* on a theoretical level rather than on a realistic one.

However, casting was not Wilder's only problem. Universal, still smarting from the failure of *W.C. Fields and Me* (1976) and *Gable and Lombard* (1976), decided against making another movie about Hollywood; then, in April 1977, Wilder left Universal. It was 1934 again, with Wilder peddling *Fedora* all over Hollywood but without success. Billy Wilder, who once saw *The Apartment* win five Academy Awards, was forced to look elsewhere for backing. He found it in Germany with Geria Films, a tax shelter of Bavaria Studios Munich. Next came the matter of distribution. Allied Artists originally planned to release *Fedora*, but it ran into problems with Lorimar Productions, the German company's U.S. agent, over distribution and booking procedures. Lorimar wanted widespread release and multiple openings; Allied Artists, concerned about the mixed reception *Fedora* received at previews, preferred an exclusive run policy. Finally, United Artists picked up *Fedora* and released it in the United States in the spring of 1979—a year and a half after it was finished.

Fedora (1978)

As a train pulls into a Paris suburb, a woman in a cape hurls herself in front of it. Someone cries, "Fedora!" Cut to Arlene Francis, who plays herself in the film, as do Henry Fonda and Michael York; as did Hedda Hopper, Cecil B. De Mille, Buster Keaton, H. B. Warner, and Anna Q. Nilsson in *Sunset Boulevard*. Ms. Francis faces a television camera and solemnly informs the world that Fedora is dead; Fedora, who was part Garbo, part Dietrich, all myth. As mourners file around Fedora's coffin that lies in the great hall of her Paris mansion, the credits begin. The music should be familiar to those who remember television's "Mama" from the early 1950s; it is Grieg's tearfully dignified "The Last Spring" that always ended the program. Among the mourners is movie producer Barry Detweiler, played by William Holden—his face now a hide of bisecting lines.

Wilder expects us to make a connection not only between *Fedora* and *Sunset Boulevard*, but also between Detweiler and Gillis. However, the casting of Holden in the role created a peculiar form of irony. Marthe Keller could not play the aged Fedora, but she could play Antonia, Antonia cosmetically aged some thirty years to resemble Fedora, and Fedora as she was in her heyday. On the other hand, Holden could not play the young Detweiler in the 1947 flashback; Wilder had to use another actor, Stephen Collins. Yet Marthe Keller could play the young Fedora in the 1947 flashback.

The casting with its ironic implications becomes a metaphor for contemporary Hollywood, where the only star in *Fedora* with a mythic personality is too old to play the same character in a thirty-year flashback. No lighting or makeup could iron out Holden's wrinkles or plane the jowls. But this was exactly the point Wilder was making by casting Holden in the part. In the Hollywood controlled by "kids with beards," there are no longer any numinous personalities. The stars who are still alive have seen their mythologies created and codified in their movies. There are no new myths to create because there are no new stars to embody them.

From the discussion thus far, it is apparent that, in *Fedora*, plot is less important than it is in any other Wilder film. The revelation comes almost at midpoint—a fact that has bothered some critics and audiences who like climactic disclosures. But Fedora's identity is not the point of the film. *Fedora* is about myth-making, Hollywood style. To be a star, one must acquire a mythology. But this was only possible when movies were a mass medium and a steady output of films could create that mythology and perpetuate it. However, the principle of perpetuation no longer applies in a Hollywood where movies are not the mass medium, where the gods and goddesses of the screen have been enshrined as a permanent pantheon, and where the myths have been immortalized on celluloid. In the past, a mythic type was kept in existence by selective replacement. Every studio had its blonde Venus; the mythic category remained although its avatars changed. At Twentieth Century–Fox, for example, Alice Faye was replaced by Betty Grable, who then gave way to Marilyn Monroe, with Jayne Mansfield waiting in the wings. But even the replacement theory is no longer applicable; Grable, Monroe, and Mansfield are dead; Alice Faye lives in semiretirement.

Fedora, then, is an anachronism. Although the film is set in the late 1970s, it is arguing for a principle that is inapplicable to the late 1970s. The myths have been made, the icons established. The studios are mere names; Universal, Warner Bros., United Artists, and Paramount have been acquired by conglomerates. There is still a Paramount on Marathon Street, but it is not Wilder's Paramount. There is still the Paramount logo; but the snow-capped mountain now reads "Gulf + Western." Gulf + Western absorbed Paramount in 1966. Today, there is a Paramount Pictures Corporation, a unit of Gulf + Western's Leisure Time Group which also includes Simon & Schuster, the publishers; Paramount television, which is responsible for such series as "Happy Days" and "Laverne and Shirley"; and the Madison Square Garden Corporation sports complex.

Wilder should have made a film like *Fedora* back in 1949 when the studio system was at least in its sunset. In 1977, the studios had even passed their twilight and were receding into the darkness. *Sunset Boulevard* could easily have been made in the late 1970s with Norma as a star of the 1940s trying to return to the screen when the industry is controlled by the "kids with beards," as Detweiler calls them.

Regardless, *Fedora* is the companion piece of *Sunset Boulevard*.

In *Sunset Boulevard*, a woman must rejuvenate herself before returning to the screen; in *Fedora*, a woman must age thirty years before returning to the screen. One transformation is an ironic commentary on the other. Norma must submit herself to chin straps, mud packs, massages, and steam baths until her body sheds excess years as well as pounds. Antonia must undergo a reverse transformation; although she is only about thirty, she must acquire that ageless look that great stars have even at sixty. In both cases, transformation leads to death. Norma and the real Fedora are alive at the end; Gillis and Antonia are not. Myth-making takes its toll even on those who helped make the myth.

Given the affinities that exist between both films, one would expect the William Holden character to narrate *Fedora*. But Detweiler is only one of the narrators. Structurally, *Fedora* is a web of flashbacks, one of them being a flashback within a flashback. Detweiler cannot narrate the entire film, as Gillis did *Sunset Boulevard*, because he only discovers in mid-film that the ethereally beautiful corpse is not Fedora. Thus, he can only tell what he knows; how he went to Corfu to persuade Fedora to do a remake of *Anna Karenina* to be called *The Snows of Yesteryear*; and how he and Fedora once had a brief affair in 1947.

The woman Detweiler saw at Corfu was Antonia, who has now become Fedora; the real Fedora, hideously disfigured, is known as the Countess Sobryanski. When one first sees Antonia/Fedora, she is at the top of the stairs in her villa. Her sun hat dominates the frame; she puts on her gloves as if she were sheathing her hands. One is clearly in the presence of a woman who has learned all the tricks of concealing the effects of time. Antonia would not have to resort to such camouflage; but Fedora must. Detweiler does not actually see her face; she is wearing dark glasses. He reminds her of the gondola-shaped golden bed (presumably the twin of Norma's) where Robert Taylor made love to her. Later, Detweiler writes her a letter recalling the time they met in 1947 on the set of *Leda and the Swan*; he was an assistant director at MGM and she was the star who, in one scene, had to appear in a pool wearing nothing but three strategically placed water lilies.

Such references make it obvious that *Fedora*, unlike Wilder's other films, is antirealistic. Despite MGM's penchant for the baroque as revealed in musicals such as *Yolanda and the Thief*

(1945) and *Ziegfeld Follies* (1946), Louis B. Mayer would never
have sanctioned a movie in 1947 about a mortal woman impreg-
nated by a god disguised as a swan. *Leda and the Swan* is an
anachronism in a movie that itself is an anachronism. Perhaps that
was the point; the other alternative is that Wilder was deliberately
trying to throw the movie buffs off the track. Who, for example,
was the model for Fedora? Garbo? Dietrich? Fedora's legs were
insured for a million dollars; only one star enjoyed that distinction—Betty Grable. Fedora is not any one star; she *is* star.

The first flashback ends with Detweiler's reading about Fedora's
death; the scene dissolves to a high shot of Fedora lying in her
casket. One should remember that the flashbacks are out of
chronology, like those in *Citizen Kane* (1941). Dates are purely
relative in *Fedora* except for 1947 and 1962, the year Fedora went
into seclusion on Corfu. One should consider the main action of
Fedora as taking place in 1977, just as the main action of the novella
was set in 1975. Thus, all Detweiler can narrate are his visit to Corfu
in 1977, also the year of Fedora's death; and the night he spent with
her on the beach at Santa Monica in 1947.

The remaining flashbacks will be narrated by the Countess
Sobryanski; Balfour, her secretary; and the Count. Actually, this is
the only way that would make any sense since each knows
something the others do not. For the flashbacks, Wilder returns to
the technique he used in *The Lost Weekend* and *The Seven Year
Itch*—the pan (tilt)-dissolve. When the Countess begins her
flashback, Wilder pan-dissolves from her face to a shot of a nurse
racing down the stairs in a clinic where, in 1962, the real Fedora
underwent cosmetic surgery that left her face disfigured. The
flashback ends with Balfour screaming "Butcher!" at the doctor as
the scene dissolves to the great hall where Detweiler lights a
cigarette for the Countess.

Next comes the Count's flashback; his is in two parts. More
objective than the Countess, he can describe the way Fedora
neglected her daughter by sending her off to boarding school. He
can also tell of Antonia's reconciliation with her mother after each
of them had experienced a personal tragedy—Antonia, an abor-
tion; Fedora, disfigurement.

The Countess begins the second round of flashbacks, telling of
her retirement to Corfu and the removal of all the mirrors from her

villa. Like any good storyteller, Wilder tries to delay the revelation as long as he can; but since the revelation and the denouement are not the same, there will be an interval between them. To Wilder, how Antonia became Fedora is not as important as what happened to Antonia after she became Fedora.

The Countess explains the origins of the great impersonation. When Henry Fonda wired that he was coming as president of the Academy of Motion Picture Arts and Sciences to award Fedora a special Oscar, Fedora conceives the idea of perpetuating her myth by having Antonia impersonate her. Apparently, Fedora had no wish to look the way Mary Pickford did—like a vandalized doll—when she received her special Oscar in 1976. Antonia would therefore accept the award; and Fonda would return to Holly-wood with stories about the ageless Fedora—which is exactly what happens.

The final flashbacks belong to Balfour and the Count since they were privy to events to which the Countess was not. Fedora is a star again, filming *The Last Waltz* in London. Since Balfour was with her in London, she is the logical choice to narrate the flashback. Balfour is left of frame; the camera pans left to right, dissolving into the set of *The Last Waltz*. Fedora has fallen in love with her leading man, Michael York. Antonia could have an affair with her costar; Fedora cannot. "You are now Fedora," Balfour impresses upon the distraught Antonia. As the scene dissolves back to the coffin, the camera reverses direction and pans right to left.

The Count then describes the repercussions of the impersona-tion; Antonia became a drug addict and had to be confined to a clinic. Finally, Balfour relates the details of her death. Emulating the heroine of *Anna Karenina*, one of her mother's greatest films and the one Detweiler wanted her to remake, Antonia threw herself in front of an approaching train. It was Balfour's voice, then, that was heard calling "Fedora!" at the beginning of the film. A pan-dissolve returns the action to the hall where the Countess is preparing for the next wave of mourners. Still thinking in theatrical terms, she asks that the coffin be moved upstage so Fedora can benefit from the soft afternoon light. "The legend must go on," the Countess insists. When Detweiler notes that the story of Fedora would make a better movie than *Anna Karenina*, the Countess replies: "But who would you get to play it?"

Her line sums up the history of *Fedora* as well as the film itself. Who can play a star in an era of non-stars? Even if, by some astral fluke, Hollywood returned to a World War II production schedule and remade the classics, who would recreate the roles? There are many competent actresses around, and Marthe Keller is one of them. But *Fedora* does not require an actress so much as a personality; Marthe Keller is not a personality.

Fedora is also Wilder's reminder to the "kids with beards" that there was a Hollywood before they came on the scene with their zoom lenses and hand-held cameras; that there was succession through replacement; and that there was a pantheon with a hierarchy of gods, goddesses, and demigods. Exactly what the new generation of filmmakers can do about a situation they did not create is problematical. Still, one hopes they will appreciate the irony of Antonia's having to age—and age convincingly—to keep Fedora's legend alive; stars generally do the opposite, even resorting to plastic surgery, to maintain the semblance of youth. In the past, stars aged cosmetically not to make a comeback, but to play a role. What Antonia does to return Fedora to films is what actresses have done *in* films—Bette Davis advancing from maidenhood to middle age in *Mr. Skeffington* (1944), and Olivia de Havilland doing the same in *To Each His Own* (1946); Barbara Stanwyck, at thirty, playing the mother of Anne Shirley in *Stella Dallas* (1937), although she was only about ten years older than Miss Shirley; Irene Dunne, made rotund and round-faced for Queen Victoria in *The Mudlark* (1950).

"Magic time," Detweiler remarks as he leaves the hall. To Wilder, this is exactly what the movies were. Yet, even in his seventies, Wilder continues to work. Although he repeats themes, motifs, and even shots, it is all part of the process of renewal. The changes in the industry have saddened but not embittered him. *Fedora* is not an angry film, nor is it an ugly one; it is an autumnal reflection on Hollywood's past—a past that, for all its excesses, gave America the only mythology it ever had.

What has kept Wilder working for fifty years in an industry where a decade is all many of its members can manage, is his double vision of reality. One likes to think of Wilder as having a Janus face where the jaundiced eye winks at the jocund one; and sometimes the eyes cross and peer at each other. In Wilder, cynicism is undercut by sentiment; and sentiment suddenly turns sardonic.

There are two Billy Wilders. The critics have called them the cynic and the sentimentalist; biographically, it would be more accurate to talk of the Viennese Wilder and Wilder the Berliner. The Viennese likes his coffee served the way it is in Vienna's coffee houses—*Kaffee mit schlag*, coffee crowned with a swirl of whipped cream. The Berliner prefers his coffee hot and black. Similarly, there is the Wilder of the waltz and the Wilder of the tango. There is the "Did they or didn't they?" Wilder, and there is the Wilder who proclaims, "Yes, they did; and they did it lustily, greedily"—the way Jan Sterling devoured an apple in *The Big Carnival*; or the way Gloria Swanson pulled William Holden down on her Viking ship bed to celebrate the New Year in *Sunset Boulevard*.

It might be possible to reconcile the two Wilders with a movie simile. Watching a Billy Wilder film is like entering one of those Warner Bros. diners where the truckers lean over the counter and tease Ann Sheridan about her "classy chassis." One orders a coffee; or, as George Raft would say, a cup of java. A steaming mug arrives, but on its bitter, black surface is a dollop of whipped cream—*Kaffee mit Schlag*, Wilder style.

Afterword

IN MANY OF the arts, there is the occasional end-of-career masterpiece. The theater, for example, can boast of *Oedipus at Colonus*, produced posthumously but written when Sophocles was ninety; *The Tempest*, which was first performed in 1611—five years before Shakespeare's death; and *Faust*, the first part of which Goethe completed in 1808 when he was 59, and the second in 1831 when he was 82. Verdi stunned operagoers with *Otello* and *Falstaff*, composed at 74 and 80, respectively. In painting, one thinks of Rembrandt's astonishing self-portraits, especially the one he did in 1669, the year of his death; and *Laocoön*, which El Greco painted a few years before he died in 1614. In poetry there is the case of Virgil: if his deathbed request (that his unrevised epic be destroyed) had been granted, he would only have been known as a bucolic poet and not as the author of the *Aeneid*. And, speaking of epics, one should not forget that the 75-year-old William Carlos Williams brought his own to completion when Book V of *Patterson* was published in 1958. The supreme example is, of course, Mozart, who, in the last year of his life (1791), completed *The Magic Flute* and composed the Clarinet Concerto with its haunting Adagio; only the monumental *Requiem* was left unfinished.

In film, the situation is quite different; it is almost as if a director is expected to end his career the same way the world ends for Eliot's hollow men: "not with a bang but a whimper." Perhaps it is that film, unlike theatre and opera, is a mass medium, subject to greater permutations of taste and technological change. Sound irrevocably changed the way movies would be

169

made; if D.W. Griffith could not adjust to the sound era, it was that sound called for an entirely different approach to filmmaking—the screenplay as opposed to the scenario. Acclimation was impossible for someone like Griffith, who lived in the past. Directors who had their own stock company often failed to understand that their actors might not always be able to make the transition from one era to another but, rather, might have to survive in other ways. Griffith's best known actress, Lillian Gish, was never the star in talkies that she was in the silents. With the coming of sound she had to settle for character roles, which she always performed faultlessly, even if it meant appearing in such films as *Miss Susie Slagle's* (1946) and *Duel in the Sun* (1947). Leading roles were available only in the theatre and on television. Widescreen posed a different set of problems for directors used to the rectangular screen. While Raoul Walsh could—and did—film in CinemaScope and Panavision, movies like *Battle Cry* (1955) and *Marines, Let's Go* (1961) will never equal *High Sierra* (1941) and *White Heat* (1949).

The nature of the industry—in which technology, film content, and acting styles often underwent radical change—prevented Hollywood's best directors from ending their careers on an impressive note, much less with a masterpiece. One thinks of D.W. Griffith's *The Struggle* (1931), Frank Capra's *Pocketful of Miracles* (1961), John Ford's *Seven Women* (1966), William Wyler's *The Liberation of L.B. Jones* (1970), and Alfred Hitchcock's *Family Plot* (1976). With Wilder it was *Buddy Buddy* (MGM, 1981).

Had *Fedora* been Wilder's *envoi* to the movies, it would have been a fitting coda—a signature film that summed up his major themes and paid homage to the studio system that nurtured his talent. When *Fedora* failed to find an audience, Wilder was more determined than ever to find a property for a comeback film. Thus, one can understand his eagerness to remake the French movie *A Pain in the A—* (1974). The plot would have allowed Wilder, who had grown even more cynical after the failure of *Fedora*, to cast a cold eye at a theme he had been exploring since *Double Indemnity*: male bonding.

A Pain in the A— depicted the unlikely relationship between a professional assassain and a suicidal husband. On paper, *Buddy*

Buddy, as the remake was called, seemed an ideal vehicle for Wilder's favorite buddies, Walter Matthau and Jack Lemmon—Matthau as Trabucco, the hit man hired by the mob to kill an informant before he testifies; and Lemmon as Victor Clooney, a television censor who ends up in the same Southern California hotel as Trabucco. Each has selected the hotel for a different reason: Clooney, to kill himself; Trabucco, to kill the informant as he enters the courthouse across the street.

While there had been an element of tenderness in the friendships in *Double Indemnity*, *The Fortune Cookie*, and *The Private Life of Sherlock Holmes*, there was none in *Buddy Buddy*. In fact, except for the subject matter, there is no trace of Wilder the *auteur* in this inexpensively produced and visually unappealing film. Taking full advantage of what, in 1981, guaranteed an "R" rating (bare breasts, "fuck" used more than once), Wilder could not resist mocking a world from which he had grown estranged. Victor's wife, Cecilia (Paula Prentiss), seeking the ultimate orgasm, enters a sex clinic where she becomes infatuated with the director (Klaus Kinski), whom she eventually leaves for a female receptionist. Victor and Trabucco encounter two hippies, a high-flying male and his pregnant significant other; when the baby is born, the father passes out joints instead of cigars.

Fads and faddists, however, are not Wilder's prime targets; he can be just as unsympathetic to the other extreme, as represented by the right-wing Victor, who cannot bring himself to say "penis" and instead refers to the "P word."

As expected, Victor, not Trabucco, ends up killing the informant. Trabucco manages to flee to a South Seas island where, inevitably, Victor, now a fugitive from the law, turns up. Twenty years earlier, when Wilder was feeling more benign, theirs could have been the beginning of a beautiful friendship, like Rick's and Renault's in *Casablanca* (1942). But Wilder's vision had grown bleaker. Trabucco, by no means happy to see Victor, realizes he "owes" him and must therefore tolerate his presence. The two become another odd couple—misogynistic males, too sexless for passion and too self-absorbed for friendship. Supposedly, they will spend their days being served by topless native women attending to their needs—fanning, feeding, and accomodating them. Matthau and Lemmon did not know it at the time, but they were really doing a run-through for *Grumpy Old Men* (1993).

Wilder was never a woman's director like Edmund Goulding and George Cukor. However, with the right property (e.g., *Double Indemnity, Sunset Boulevard, Fedora*), he could make women, who might otherwise emerge as freaks, into human beings worthy of understanding, if not empathy. In *Double Indemnity* Phyllis does love Neff—in her fashion—although, at the end, she denies it. Her denial is really a confession of her own self-loathing, resulting from a past she would rather forget and a marriage she chose to dissolve by murder. That Phyllis and Neff are both motivated by money and sex may not make them especially endearing. Yet Wilder makes it clear that each had a spark of decency that never caught fire. The love-death that ends the film has a kind of perverse romanticism: ex-lovers squaring off because each was unable to live up to the other's expectations. The combination of cynicism and tenderness with which MacMurray and Stanwyck played the scene, and Wilder's refusal to reduce Phyllis to a murderous vamp, resulted in a *femme noire* who has often been imitated (e.g., the murder-minded women in *Dead Reckoning* [1974], *The Lady from Shanghai* [1948], *Too Late for Tears* [1949], and *Human Desire* [1954]). But no filmmaker has ever succeeded in making a sleazy male and a woman, who admits she is "rotten to the heart," so thoroughly believable. Part of the credit belongs to Wilder the screenwriter and Chandler his collaborator; the rest to Stanwyck, MacMurray, and Wilder the director.

In *Buddy Buddy* Wilder was dealing with two characters far less alienating than the *Double Indemnity* pair. Yet Trabucco and Victor seem much worse; one almost wishes Victor would kill himself and Trabucco be caught. How different it was in *The Apartment*, when audiences hoped Fran's suicide attempt would not prove fatal (it didn't); or, in *The Private Life of Sherlock Holmes*, that Ilsa, the German spy, would not be apprehended (she was). In these films Wilder cared about his characters; in *Buddy Buddy*, however, he might have cared initially, but then gave up and settled for caricature. How Trabucco and Victor became what they are is never explained, and when no explanation is forthcoming, disinterest—and eventually apathy—set in.

That *Buddy Buddy* was Wilder's last collaboration with I.A.L. Diamond, who died of cancer in 1988, is an ironic commentary on one of Hollywood's most enduring friendships. One would rather think of Wilder and Diamond as Neff and Keyes rather than Trabucco and Victor. At least Neff got an "I love you" from Keyes; all Victor got from Trabucco was fantasy island. Despite its relative brevity (96 minutes), *Buddy Buddy* seems longer. The film has a tired quality, as if everyone, including Wilder, had run out of energy. Part of the problem is the casting: Matthau, Lemmon, and Prentiss—at 61, 56, and 44 respectively—were simply too old for their parts. In Wilder's case, however, the reason does not seem to have been age, although he was 75. Wilder had energy to spare when he did *Fedora* three years earlier. More likely, it was his inability to temper his contempt for what he was satirizing which resulted in a singularly unfunny movie. Perhaps it is best to think of *Buddy Buddy* as the equivalent of the Greek satyr play. In the dramatic festivals, three tragedies would be followed by a satyr play—a rowdy farce that would offer the audience a respite from four or five hours of human suffering. Certainly if Euripides' reputation rested on his only surviving satyr play, *The Cyclops*—and not on such masterpieces as *Medea*, *Hippolytus*, *The Trojan Women*, and *The Bacchae*—he would only be a footnote in the history of drama.

Ironically, Wilder's inability to adjust to postmodernism worked in his favor. His career ended at a time when he was eligible for elder statesman—which meant a succession of tributes, honors, and retrospectives as America grew more conscious of its film heritage. The Film Society of Lincoln Center did not hold *Buddy Buddy* against Wilder; a year later, on 3 May 1982, the Society paid tribute to Wilder, as it had earlier to Charlie Chaplin, Alfred Hitchcock, Barbara Stanwyck, Bob Hope, and George Cukor. In 1986 Wilder was the recipient of the American Film Institute's fourteenth annual Life Achievement Award; a year later the Academy of Motion Picture Arts and Sciences singled him out for the Irving G. Thalberg Memorial Award. In 1990 the John F. Kennedy Center of the Performing Arts honored Wilder along with Katharine Hepburn, Dizzy Gillespie, Rise Stevens, and Jule Stein. The following year, Wilder was the subject of a retrospective at New York's Film Forum. In 1993 President Clinton awarded him the National Medal of Arts; in 1994, when Sir Andrew Lloyd Weber's musical version of *Sunset Boulevard*, with book and lyrics by Don Black and Christopher Hampton, opened on Broadway, the playbill credit, "Based on the Billy Wilder Film," was unnecessary. The screenplay had come to the stage virtually intact—right down to such classic lines as "I am big! It's the pictures that got small," which have now entered the Hollywood Book of Quotations.

Wilder had every reason to be proud of the musical's success: the book was really his. Anyone adapting *Sunset Boulevard* for the musical stage had only to copy the film. Wilder has always considered himself a writer who moved behind the camera; in short, a writer-director. The hyphen merely created a dual title without emphasizing one over the other. Thus, for one who began as a writer and continued to perceive himself as one after he turned to directing, receiving the Career Achievement Award from the Writers Guild Foundation in 1995, on the eve of his ninetieth birthday, was true recognition, especially since Wilder had not had a screenplay credit for fourteen years.

Since Wilder has worked with some true screen icons, celebrity biographers researching the lives of Marlene Dietrich, Humphrey Bogart, William Holden, Audrey Hepburn, and Marilyn Monroe must seek him out. Thus, when Donald Spoto was gathering material for his definitive biography of Marilyn Monroe (New York: HarperCollins, 1993), he was able to get Wilder to admit that, despite his problems with the star, she had "a natural instinct for how to read a comic line." Wilder also gave what, to him, was the ultimate comparison: "She had a quality no one else ever had on the screen except Garbo."

Academics also began to pay closer attention to Wilder's art. Despite the omission of *Fedora*, Leland Poague's *The Hollywood Professionals: Billy Wilder and Leo McCarey* (San Diego: A.S. Barnes, 1980) is a detailed examination of Wilder's films, concluding that they are the work of a major director. The one Wilder film that continues to attract scholars is *Double Indemnity* because it has entered the canon of film noir. Yet Wilder would have preferred the screenplay to take precedence over genre. When screenwriter Robert Blees interviewed Barbara Stanwyck for *American Film* (April 1987), she admitted *Double Indemnity* was the most perfect script she ever read. However, *Double In-*

demnity belongs to that *annus mirabilis*, 1944 (which also saw the release of *Murder, My Sweet* and *Laura*, other noirs to which *Double Indemnity* is superior); thus it is considered either noir or pre-noir, depending on whether noir is regarded as an ongoing refinement of expressionistic cinema or a new genre that emerged after World War II.

That Wilder was thinking "noir" as early as 1943 suggests that there were directors who were inclined to expose the "dark" side of American life before an Allied victory. One of the most intriguing studies of *Double Indemnity* is Ruth Prigozy's "*Double Indemnity*: Billy Wilder's *Crime and Punishment*" (*Literature/Film Quarterly* 12 [1984]: 160-70), which argues that Wilder, whose mother, grandmother, and stepfather were Holocaust victims, conceived *Double Indemnity* (perhaps unconsciously) as a reflection of a mentality (the conscious abrogation of moral standards to achieve a self-serving end) that was not dissimilar to the Third Reich's. Prigozy reminds us that Wilder planned to end the film with Neff's going to the gas chamber, even spending $150,000 to shoot the sequence. However, Paramount intervened, claiming the death quotient in the film was high enough; even Wilder concurred.

There are, of course, other ways of looking at *Double Indemnity*. Since Raymond Chandler shared screenplay credit with Wilder, anyone writing on Chandler would first have to compare the script with James M. Cain's novel, and then place *Double Indemnity* within the context of Chandler's screen work, as William Luhr has done in *Raymond Chandler and Film* (New York: Ungar, 1982). But as film noir, *Double Indemnity* includes the familiar figure of the *femme noire*, the lethal lady who entraps her unsuspecting victim. Thus feminist criticism will take a different approach to the film—e.g., Claire Johnston's "*Double Indemnity*" (in *Women in Film Noir*, ed. E. Ann Kaplan [London: British Film Institute, 1978]: 100-11). The one article on *Double Indemnity* that examines the film's production history, imagery, and fatalism and best explains why it is the archetypal film noir is James Naremore's "Making and Remaking *Double Indemnity*" (*Film Comment* 32 [January/February 1996]: 22-31).

As an immigrant, Wilder was part of a Hollywood group that included Fritz Lang, Bertolt Brecht, Jean Renoir, Aldous Huxley,

Alfred Hithcock, etc. On that curious circle, see Anthony Heilbut, *Exiled in Paradise* (New York: Viking, 1983), and John Russell Taylor, *Strangers in Paradise: The Hollywood Emigres 1933–1950* (New York: Holt, 1983).

Clearly, much has changed since the 1980 publication of this book. Wilder's reputation has reached such heights that the Special Collector's Issue of *Entertainment Weekly* (March 1996), basically a guide to the Oscars, included a profile on Wilder, who had not made a movie in fifteen years. Steve Daly's piece, simply entitled "Billy Wilder," is, as the cover claims, a tribute—a tribute to a man who could behave autocratically on the set but who eventually provided his cast with a script that may not have always been complete on the first day of shooting but eventually reflected the way he heard the characters speak as well as the way his actors did. Tony Curtis's theory that, in a Wilder film, the script did the directing is the ultimate compliment to a man who could wear two hats at the same time and never be overdressed.

Even a director of Sydney Pollack's stature (*They Shoot Horses, Don't They?* [1972], *The Way We Were* [1975], *Tootsie* [1985], *Out of Africa* [1990], etc.) had reservations about remaking *Sabrina*. Although Pollack eventually did the 1995 remake, he at first demurred: "I certainly didn't want to do a remake of a Billy Wilder movie—he's such . . . an icon" (*Hollywood Reporter*, 13 December 1995: 12).

Small wonder that Pollack would call Wilder an icon. The National Film Registry, established by the Library of Congress in 1988 to single out and preserve historically significant films, includes four of Wilder's: *Double Indemnity*, *Sunset Boulevard*, *Some Like It Hot*, and *The Apartment*. Hitchcock has the same number (*Shadow of a Doubt*, *Psycho*, *North by Northwest*, and *Vertigo*); only John Ford has more: five (*Stagecoach*, *The Grapes of Wrath*, *How Green Was My Valley*, *My Darling Clementine*, and *The Searchers*). It is not surprising that, of all of Wilder's films, these four made it into the Registry. Each represents Wilder's ability to translate complex subject matters (infidelity and murder, self-delusion and murder, crossdressing and gender-bending, infidelity and deception) into commercially and artistically successful films.

As Wilder progressed from contract director to *auteur* to icon, the industry to which he devoted his life underwent a metamorphosis of its own. Video is here for the duration. Except for Films, Inc., the 16 mm. distributors listed in the filmography no longer exist. In addition, Billy Wilder's Paramount is now a subsidiary of Viacom, the owner of Blockbuster Video, which, one hopes, will see that its stores continue to stock the films of one of Paramount's—and Hollywood's—greatest directors.

Notes and References

Chapter One

1. According to Maurice Zolotow, *Billy Wilder in Hollywood* (New York, 1977), p. 41, the number may be closer to 200, including ghost-written scripts.

2. For the complete list, see "Dialogue on Film: Billy Wilder and I. A. L. Diamond," *American Film*, July-August 1976, p. 44; for synopses and credits, see Steve Seidman, *The Film Career of Billy Wilder* (Boston, 1977), pp. 39–49.

3. Exactly how much Wilder contributed to *Menschen am Sonntag* has yet to be determined; see Andrew Sarris, "Billy Wilder: Closet Romanticist," *Film Comment*, July-August 1976, p. 8.

4. Despite his importance, little has been written on Dreier except for Léon Barsacq, *Caligari's Cabinet and Other Grand Illusions* (Boston, 1976), pp. 62–63; 205; and Mary Corliss and Carlos Clarens, "Designed for Film: The Hollywood Art Director," *Film Comment*, May-June 1978, pp. 48–49.

5. Herman G. Weinberg, *The Lubtisch Touch: A Critical Study* (New York, 1968), p. 171.

6. *The Hollywood Hallucination* (New York, 1970), p. 86.

7. Corliss and Clarens (above, n. 4, p. 31).

Chapter Three

1. Little is known of the play, even whether it was written in Hungarian or English. It was never performed on Broadway, according to Emro J. Gergely, *Hungarian Drama in New York: American Adaptations 1908–1940* (Philadelphia, 1947), p. 6.

179

2. On their stormy collaboration see Frank MacShane, *The Life of Raymond Chandler* (New York, 1976), pp. 106–13; Ivan Moffat, "On the Fourth Floor of Paramount: Interview with Billy Wilder," in Miriam Gross, ed., *The World of Raymond Chandler* (New York, 1978), pp. 44–51.

3. The screenplay is available in John Gassner and Dudley Nichols, ed., *Best Film Plays 1945* (New York, 1977).

Chapter Four

1. In his otherwise exemplary *The Film Career of Billy Wilder* (Boston, 1977), pp. 11–12, Steve Seidman claims that Paramount changed the title from *The Big Carnival* to *Ace in the Hole*. Other Wilder scholars say the opposite. The proposed title was *The Human Interest*; then it became *Ace in the Hole*. The *Bulletin of Screen Achievement Records* (January 10, 1952) shows that the title was changed from *Ace in the Hole* to *The Big Carnival*.

Chapter Five

1. The text is available in *Molnár's Romantic Comedies: Eight Plays by Ferenc Molnár* (New York, 1952).

Chapter Six

1. The novel does not seem to have been translated into English.

Chapter Seven

1. "It's a Long Way to Oxyrhynchus," *Spectator*, July 7, 1971, p. 9.

2. According to Stanley Kauffmann, *Living Images: Film Comment and Criticism* (New York, 1975), p. 366, *Some Like It Hot* was inspired by a German film, *Fanfares of Love*, of which little is known except that it involved two male musicians who joined an all-girl band.

Chapter Eight

1. On the whole controversy, see Jack Vizzard, *See No Evil: Life inside a Hollywood Censor* (New York, 1970), pp. 300–307.

2. A French translation entitled *L'heure éblouissante* was published in *Paris Théatre* 71 (April 1953): 13–58. Wilder probably read it in French or saw the Paris production since the working title of *Kiss Me, Stupid* was *The Dazzling Hour*, which is the literal translation of *L'heure éblouissante*.

Chapter Nine

1. Parker Tyler, who wrote so perceptively about the Neff-Keyes relationship in *Magic and Myth of the Movies* (New York, 1970), pp. 175–89, began to see homosexuality where it never existed; see his *Screening the Sexes: Homosexuality in the Movies* (New York, 1972), p. 344; Stephen Farber, "The Films of Billy Wilder," *Film Comment*, Winter 1971–72, p. 16, writes that "homosexuality plays a furtive role in a number of [Wilder's] films."

Chapter Eleven

1. Sir Arthur Conan Doyle, *The Complete Sherlock Holmes* (New York, 1930), p. 158.
2. Michael Pointer, *The Sherlock Holmes File* (New York, 1976), p. 63.
3. Derek Elley, "The Film Composer: Miklós Rózsa (Part Two)," *Films and Filming*, June 1977, pp. 33–34.
4. Charles Higham, *The Adventures of Conan Doyle: The Life and Creator of Sherlock Holmes* (New York, 1976), pp. 230–32.
5. For some reason the film is included under "Homosexuality" in Leslie Halliwell's exhaustive *The Filmgoer's Companion*, 6th ed. (New York, 1978), p. 350.

Chapter Twelve

1. Wilder originally planned to open *Sunset Boulevard* in a morgue where approximately eight corpses, including the narrator, told each other the circumstances that led to their deaths. Wilder claimed this sequence contained "some of the best material I've ever shot," according to Charles Higham and Joel Greenberg, ed., *The Celluloid Muse* (New York, 1972), p. 284.
2. See Shirley MacLaine's comments in Maurice Zolotow, *Billy Wilder in Hollywood* (New York, 1977), pp. 336–39.
3. Garson Kanin, *Hollywood* (New York, 1974), p. 178.

4. On the *Fedora* ordeal, see Rex McGee, "The Life and Hard Times of *Fedora*," *American Film*, February 1979, pp. 17–21, 30–32.

5. In a letter dated September 24, 1979, Kathleen Morell, secretary to Universal vice-president Verna Fields, clarified Wilder's status at the studio where he was housed between September 1973 and April 1977. He was not under contract to Universal for that entire period. Wilder was included in a production-distribution arrangement (September 4, 1973) to collaborate on the screenplay of *The Front Page* and direct it for Universal. He was then involved in a contract (March 16, 1976) to prepare a screenplay of *Fedora*. The project was dropped on November 19, 1976, and Wilder left Universal in early April 1977. Ms. Morell agrees that between the filming of *The Front Page* and the development of the *Fedora* project, "he was indeed a 'visiting professor.'"

Selected Bibliography

1. Screenplays

BRACKETT, CHARLES, and WILDER, BILLY. *The Lost Weekend.* In *Best Film Plays 1945.* Ed. John Gassner and Dudley Nichols. New York: Garland, 1977.

———, and REISCH, WALTER. *Ninotchka.* The MGM Library of Film Scripts. New York: Viking, 1972.

CHANDLER, RAYMOND, and WILDER, BILLY. *Double Indemnity.* In *Best Film Plays 1945.* Ed. John Gassner and Dudley Nichols. New York: Garland, 1977.

WILDER, BILLY, and DIAMOND, I. A. L. *Some Like It Hot.* New York: Signet Books, 1959.

———. *Irma La Douce.* New York: Midwood-Tower, 1963.

———. *The Apartment and The Fortune Cookie: Two Screenplays.* New York: Praeger, 1971.

———. *The Apartment.* In *Film Scripts Three.* Ed. George P. Garrett, O. B. Hardison, Jr., and Jane R. Gelfman. New York: Appleton-Century-Crofts, 1972.

2. Interviews

DICK, BERNARD F. *Anatomy of Film.* New York: St. Martin's Press, 1978. Wilder on the auteur theory, nature of directing, changes in film industry.

McBRIDE, JOSEPH, and McCARTHY, TODD. "Going for Extra Innings." *Film Comment* 15 (January-February 1979): 40–48. A cantankerous Wilder taking issue with Zolotow's portrait of him in *Billy Wilder in Hollywood.* One of the few interviews in which Wilder is actually unpleasant.

PHILLIPS, GENE. "Interview with Billy Wilder." *Literature/Film Quarterly 4 (Winter 1975):* 3–12. Wilder reminiscing on his career.

WILDER, BILLY, and DIAMOND, I. A. L. "Dialogue on Film." *American Film*
1 (July-August 1976): 33–48. A settled Wilder, highly informative on
his sources, his working methods, and the genesis of his screenplays.

3. Books and Articles

CORLISS, RICHARD. *Talking Pictures: Screenwriters in the American
Cinema.* New York: Penguin Books, 1975. An unflatteringly biased
appraisal of Wilder's scripts and a candid but more humane assess-
ment of Brackett.

ELLEY, DEREK. "The Film Composer: Miklós Rózsa (Part Two)." *Films
and Filming* 23 (June 1977): 30–34. Extremely important for information on episodes cut from *The Private Life of Sherlock Holmes.*

FARBER, STEPHEN. "The Films of Billy Wilder." *Film Comment* 7 (Winter
1971–72): 8–22. "Idealized homoerotic experiences" in Wilder's films.

FROUG, WILLIAM. *The Screenwriter Looks at the Screenwriter.* New York:
Macmillan, 1972. I. A. L. Diamond on his relationship with Wilder.

KANIN, GARSON. *Hollywood.* New York: Viking, 1974. Brackett's version
of the break up with Wilder.

MADSEN, AXEL. *Billy Wilder.* Cinema One series. Bloomington: Indiana
University Press, 1969. The films through *The Fortune Cookie.*

McBRIDE, JOSEPH, and WILMINGTON, MICHAEL. "The Private Life of Billy
Wilder." *Film Quarterly* 23 (Summer 1970): 2–9. The sex-money-
greed syndrome in Wilder's films.

SARRIS, ANDREW. "Billy Wilder: Closet Romanticist." *Film Comment*
12 (July-August 1976): 7–9. Sarris recants, admitting he "grossly
underrated" Wilder in *The American Cinema.*

TURNER, ADRIAN, and SINYARD, NEIL, "Billy Wilder's *Fedora.*" *Sight and
Sound* 48 (Summer 1979): 160–65. A thoughtful essay that places the
film within the context of Wilder's work.

ZOLOTOW, MAURICE. *Billy Wilder in Hollywood.* New York: G. P. Putnam's
Sons, 1977. Highly readable and informative biography, marred by
some unnecessary psychoanalyzing of Wilder.

4. Bibliography

SEIDMAN, STEVE. *The Film Career of Billy Wilder.* Boston: G. K. Hall
& Co., 1977. Invaluable reference guide containing information on
whereabouts of unpublished screenplays as well as plot synopses,
credits, and an extensive annotated bibliography.

Filmography

THE MAJOR AND THE MINOR (Paramount, 1942)
Producer: Arthur Hornblow, Jr.
Screenplay: Charles Brackett, Billy Wilder, based on the story "Sunny Goes Home" by Fannie Kilbourne and the play *Connie Goes Home* by Edward Childs Carpenter
Cinematographer: Leo Tover
Art Directors: Roland Anderson, Hans Dreier
Music: Robert Emmett Dolan
Editor: Doane Harrison
Cast: Ginger Rogers (Susan Applegate), Ray Milland (Major Philip Kirby), Rita Johnson (Pamela), Robert Benchley (Mr. Osborne), Diana Lynn (Lucy)
Running Time: 100 minutes
Released: September 1942
16mm rental: Universal/16

FIVE GRAVES TO CAIRO (Paramount, 1943)
Producer: Charles Brackett
Screenplay: Charles Brackett, Billy Wilder, based on a play by Lajos Biro
Cinematographer: John F. Seitz
Art Directors: Hans Dreier, Ernst Fegete
Music: Miklós Rózsa
Editor: Doane Harrison
Cast: Franchot Tone (Bramble), Anne Baxter (Mouche), Akim Tamiroff (Farid), Peter Van Eyck (Lieutenant Schwegler), Erich von Stroheim (Rommel)
Running Time: 96 minutes
Released: May 1943
16mm rental: Universal/16

DOUBLE INDEMNITY (Paramount, 1944)
Producer: Joseph Sistrom
Screenplay: Raymond Chandler, Billy Wilder, based on the novella by
    James M. Cain
Cinematographer: John F. Seitz
Art Directors: Hans Dreier, Hal Pereira
Music: Miklós Rózsa
Editor: Doane Harrison
Cast: Fred MacMurray (Walter Neff), Barbara Stanwyck (Phyllis Die-
    trichson), Edward G. Robinson (Barton Keyes)
Running Time: 107 minutes
Released: May 1944
16mm rental: Universal/16

THE LOST WEEKEND (Paramount; 1945)
Producer: Charles Brackett
Screenplay: Charles Brackett, Billy Wilder, based on the novel by Charles
    Jackson
Cinematographer: John F. Seitz
Art Directors: Hans Dreier, Earl Hedrick
Music: Miklós Rósza
Editor: Doane Harrison
Cast: Ray Milland (Don Birnam), Jane Wyman (Helen St. James),
    Howard da Silva (Nat), Phillip Terry (Wick)
Running Time: 99 minutes
Released: November 1945
16mm rental: Universal/16

THE EMPEROR WALTZ (Paramount, 1948)
Producer: Charles Brackett
Screenplay: Charles Brackett, Billy Wilder
Cinematographer: George Barnes (in Technicolor)
Art Directors: Hans Dreier, Earl Hedrick
Music: Victor Young
Editor: Doane Harrison
Cast: Bing Crosby (Virgil Smith), Joan Fontaine (Johanna), Roland
    Culver (Baron Holenia), Richard Haydn (Emperor Franz Josef)
Running Time: 106 minutes
Released: July 1948
16mm rental: Universal/16

A FOREIGN AFFAIR (Paramount, 1948)
Producer: Charles Brackett
Screenplay: Charles Brackett, Billy Wilder, Richard L. Breen, based on an
   original story by David Shaw
Cinematographer: Charles B. Lang, Jr.
Art Directors: Hans Dreier, John Meehan
Music: Franz Waxman
Editor: Doane Harrison
Cast: Jean Arthur (Phoebe Frost), Marlene Dietrich (Erika von Schlue-
   tow), John Lund (Captain John Pringle), Millard Mitchell (Colonel
   Rufus J. Plummer)
Running Time: 116 minutes
Released: August 1948
16mm rental: Universal/16

SUNSET BOULEVARD (Paramount, 1950)
Producer: Charles Brackett
Screenplay: Charles Brackett, Billy Wilder, D. M. Marshman, Jr.
Cinematographer: John F. Seitz
Art Directors:HansDreier, John Meehan
Music: Franz Waxman
Editor: Arthur Schmidt
Cast: Gloria Swanson (Norma Desmond), William Holden (Joe Gillis),
   Erich von Stroheim (Max von Mayerling), Nancy Olson (Betty
   Schaefer), Fred Clark (Sheldrake); Cecil B. De Mille, Hedda Hopper,
   Buster Keaton, H. B. Warner, Ray Evans, Jay Livingston, Anna Q.
   Nilsson (Themselves).
Running Time: 111 minutes
Released: August 1950
16mm rental: Paramount Non-Theatrical

THE BIG CARNIVAL (ACE IN THE HOLE; Paramount, 1951)
Producer: Billy Wilder
Screenplay: Billy Wilder, Lesser Samuels, Walter Newman
Cinematographer: Charles Lang, Jr.
Art Directors: Hal Pereira, Earl Hedrick
Music: Hugo Friedhofer
Editors: Doane Harrison, Arthur Schmidt
Cast: Kirk Douglas (Chuck Tatum), Jan Sterling (Lorraine Minosa), Bob
   Arthur (Herbie), Richard Benedict (Leo Minosa), Ray Teal (Sheriff)
Running Time: 111 minutes
Released: July 1951
16mm rental: Paramount Non-Theatrical

STALAG 17 (Paramount, 1953)
Producer: Billy Wilder
Screenplay: Billy Wilder, Edwin Blum, based on the play by Donald
    Bevan and Edmund Trzcinski
Cinematographer: Ernest Laszlo
Art Directors: Hal Pereira, Franz Bachelin
Music: Franz Waxman
Editor: George Tomasini
Cast: William Holden (Sefton), Don Taylor (Dunbar), Robert Strauss
    ("Animal"), Harvey Lembeck (Harry), Otto Preminger (Oberst von
    Scherbach), Peter Graves (Price), Sig Ruman (Schulz)
Running Time: 121 minutes
Released: July 1953
16mm rental: Paramount Non-Theatrical

SABRINA (Paramount, 1954)
Producer: Billy Wilder
Screenplay: Billy Wilder, Samuel Taylor, Ernest Lehman, based on
    Samuel Taylor's play *Sabrina Fair*
Cinematographer: Charles Lang, Jr.
Art Directors: Hal Pereira, Walter Tyler
Music: Frederick Hollander
Editor: Arthur Schmidt
Cast: Humphrey Bogart (Linus Larrabee), Audrey Hepburn (Sabrina
    Fairchild), William Holden (David Larrabee), John Williams
    (Thomas Fairchild)
Running Time: 114 minutes
Released: October 1954
16mm rental: Paramount Non-Theatrical

THE SEVEN YEAR ITCH (Twentieth Century–Fox, 1955)
Producers: Charles K. Feldman, Billy Wilder
Screenplay: Billy Wilder, George Axelrod, based on the play by George
    Axelrod
Cinematographer: Milton Krasner (in CinemaScope)
Art Directors: Lyle Wheeler, George W. Davis
Music: Alfred Newman
Editor: Hugh S. Fowler
Cast: Marilyn Monroe (The Girl), Tom Ewell (Richard Sherman), Evelyn
    Keyes (Helen Sherman), Sonny Tufts (Tom McKenzie), Victor
    Moore (Plumber)

Running Time: 105 minutes
Released: June 1955
16mm rental: Films, Inc.

THE SPIRIT OF ST. LOUIS (Warner Bros., 1957)

Producer: Leland Hayward
Screenplay: Billy Wilder, Wendell Mayes, based on the book by Charles
    A. Lindbergh
Cinematographers: Robert Burks, J. Peverell Marley (in CinemaScope)
Art Director: Art Loel
Music: Franz Waxman
Cast: James Stewart (Charles A. Lindbergh), Murray Hamilton (Bud
    Gurney), Patricia Smith (Mirror Girl)
Running Time: 135 minutes
Released: April 1957
16mm rental: as yet unavailable

LOVE IN THE AFTERNOON (Allied Artists, 1957)

Producer: Billy Wilder
Screenplay: Billy Wilder, I. A. L. Diamond, based on Claude Anet's novel,
    Ariane
Cinematographer: William Mellor
Art Director: Alexander Trauner
Music: Franz Waxman
Editor: Leonid Azar
Cast: Gary Cooper (Flannagan), Audrey Hepburn (Ariane Chevasse),
    Maurice Chevalier (Claude Chevasse)
Running Time: 125 minutes
Released: June 1957
16mm rental: Hurlock Cine-World

WITNESS FOR THE PROSECUTION (United Artists, 1958)

Producer: Arthur Hornblow, Jr.
Screenplay: Billy Wilder, Harry Kurnitz, based on the play and novel by
    Agatha Christie
Cinematographer: Russell Harlan
Art Director: Alexander Trauner
Music: Matty Malneck
Editor: Daniel Mandell

Cast: Tyrone Power (Leonard Vole), Marlene Dietrich (Christine Vole),
    Charles Laughton (Sir Wilfrid Robarts), Elsa Lanchester (Miss
    Plimsoll), Una O'Connor (Janet McKenzie), Henry Daniell
    (Mayhew)
Running Time: 116 minutes
Released: February 1958
16mm rental: UA/16

SOME LIKE IT HOT (United Artists, 1959)
Producer: Billy Wilder
Screenplay: Billy Wilder, I. A. L. Diamond, suggested by an unpublished
    story by R. Thoeren and M. Logan
Cinematographer: Charles Lang, Jr.
Art Director: Ted Haworth
Music: Adolph Deutsch
Editor: Arthur Schmidt
Cast: Marilyn Monroe (Sugar), Tony Curtis (Joe), Jack Lemmon (Jerry),
    George Raft ("Spats" Colombo), Pat O'Brien (Mulligan), Joe E.
    Brown (Osgood Fielding)
Running Time: 121 minutes
Released: March 1959
16mm rental: UA/16

THE APARTMENT (United Artists, 1960)
Producer: Billy Wilder
Screenplay: Billy Wilder, I. A. L. Diamond
Cinematographer: Joseph LaShelle (Panavision)
Art Director: Alexander Trauner
Music: Adolph Deutsch
Editor: Daniel Mandell
Cast: Jack Lemmon (Bud), Shirley MacLaine (Fran Kubelik), Fred
    MacMurray (Sheldrake), Ray Walston (Dobisch), Edie Adams (Miss
    Olsen)
Running Time: 125 minutes
Released: June 1960
16mm rental: UA/16

ONE, TWO, THREE (United Artists, 1961)
Producer: Billy Wilder

Screenplay: Billy Wilder, I. A. L. Diamond, based on the one-act farce by
Ferenc Molnár.
Cinematographer: Daniel Fapp (Panavision)
Art Director: Alexander Trauner
Music: Andre Previn
Editor: Daniel Mandell
Cast: James Cagney (MacNamara), Horst Buchholz (Otto Ludwig Piffl),
Pamela Tiffin (Scarlett), Arlene Francis (Mrs. MacNamara)
Running Time: 115 minutes
Released: December 1961
16mm rental: UA/16

IRMA LA DOUCE (United Artists, 1963)
Producer: Billy Wilder
Screenplay: Billy Wilder, I. A. L. Diamond, based on the play by
Alexandre Breffort
Cinematographer: Joseph LaShelle (Panavision)
Art Director: Alexander Trauner
Music: Andre Previn (score for original stage musical by Marguerite
Monnot)
Editor: Daniel Mandell
Cast: Jack Lemmon (Nestor), Shirley MacLaine (Irma), Lou Jacobi
(Moustache)
Running Time: 147 minutes
Released: July 1963
16mm rental: UA/16

KISS ME, STUPID (United Artists, 1964)
Producer: Billy Wilder
Screenplay: Billy Wilder, I. A. L. Diamond, suggested by Anna Bonacci's
play *L'Ora della Fantasia*.
Cinematographer: Joseph LaShelle (Panavision)
Art Director: Robert Luthardt
Music: Andre Previn
Editor: Daniel Mandell
Cast: Dean Martin (Dino), Kim Novak (Polly the Pistol), Ray Walston
(Orville J. Spooner), Felicia Farr (Zelda Spooner), Cliff Osmond
(Barney Millsap).
Running Time: 124 minutes

Released: December 1964
16mm rental: UA/16

THE FORTUNE COOKIE (United Artists, 1966)
Producer: Billy Wilder
Screenplay: Billy Wilder, I. A. L. Diamond
Cinematographer: Joseph LaShelle (Panavision)
Art Director: Robert Luthardt
Music: Andre Previn
Editor: Daniel Mandell
Cast: Jack Lemmon (Harry Hinkle), Walter Matthau (Willie Gingrich),
    Ron Rich (Boom-Boom Jackson), Judi West (Sandy)
Running Time: 126 minutes
Released: November 1966
16mm rental: UA/16

THE PRIVATE LIFE OF SHERLOCK HOLMES (United Artists, 1970)
Producer: Billy Wilder
Screenplay: Billy Wilder, I. A. L. Diamond, based on characters created
    by Sir Arthur Conan Doyle
Cinematographer: Christopher Challis (Panavision)
Art Director: Tony Inglis
Music: Miklós Rózsa
Editor: Ernest Walter
Cast: Robert Stephens (Sherlock Holmes), Colin Blakely (Dr. John H.
    Watson), Christopher Lee (Mycroft Holmes), Genevieve Page
    (Gabrielle Valladon), Tamara Toumanova (Petrova)
Running Time: 125 minutes
Released: November 1970
16mm rental: UA/16

AVANTI! (United Artists, 1972)
Producer: Billy Wilder
Screenplay: Billy Wilder, I. A. L. Diamond, based on the play by Samuel
    Taylor
Cinematographer: Luigi Kuveiller (Panavision)
Art Director: Ferdinado Scarfioti
Musical Arrangements: Carlo Rustichelli
Editor: Ralph E. Winters

Cast: Jack Lemmon (Wendell Armbruster), Juliet Mills (Pamela Piggott),
Clive Revill (Carlo Carlucci)
Running Time: 144 minutes
Released: December 1972
16mm rental: UA/16

THE FRONT PAGE (Universal, 1974)
Producer: Paul Monash
Screenplay: Billy Wilder, I. A. L. Diamond, based on the play by Ben
Hecht and Charles MacArthur
Cinematographer: Jordan S. Cronewath (Panavision)
Art Directors: Henry Bumstead, Henry Larrecy
Editor: Ralph E. Winters
Cast: Jack Lemmon (Hildy Johnson), Walter Matthau (Walter Burns),
Carol Burnett (Molly), David Wayne (Bensinger), Susan Sarandon
(Peggy), Austin Pendleton (Earl Williams), Martin Gabel (Dr. Eggel-
hoffer)
Running Time: 105 minutes
Released: December 1974
16mm rental: Universal/16

FEDORA (United Artists, 1979)
Producer: Billy Wilder
Screenplay: Billy Wilder, I. A. L. Diamond, based on a story from
Crowned Heads by Thomas Tryon
Cinematographer: Gerry Fisher
Art Director: Alexander Trauner
Music: Miklós Rózsa
Editor: Stefan Arnsten
Cast: William Holden (Barry Detweiler), Marthe Keller (Fedora), Jose
Ferrer (Dr. Vando), Hans Jaray (Sobryanski); Henry Fonda, Michael
York (Themselves); Hildegard Knef (Countess Sobryanski)
Running Time: 113 minutes
Released: April 1979
16mm rental: UA/16

BUDDY BUDDY (Metro-Goldwyn-Mayer, 1981)
Producer: Jay Weston

Screenplay: Billy Wilder and I.A.L. Diamond, based on a play and story
    by Francis Veber
Director of Photography: Harry Stradling, Jr.
Production designed by Daniel A. Lomino
Music: Lalo Schifrin
Editor: Argyle Nelson
Cast: Jack Lemmon (Victor Clooney), Walter Matthau (Trabucco), Paula
    Prentiss (Celia Clooney), Klaus Kinski (Dr. Zuckerbrot), Joan Shawlee
    (Receptionist)
Running Time: 96 minutes
Released: December 1981
Available on MGM/UA Home Video

Index

Other titles of interest

THE AMERICAN CINEMA
Directors and Directions,
1929–1968
Andrew Sarris
393 pp.
0-306-80728-9 $14.95

M-G-M's GREATEST MUSICALS
The Arthur Freed Unit
Hugh Fordin
576 pp., 254 photos
0-306-80730-0 $19.95

FELIX
The Twisted Tale of the World's
Most Famous Cat
John Canemaker
192 pp., 200 drawings & photos,
8 pp. in color
0-306-80731-9 $16.95

ORSON WELLES
Revised and Expanded Edition
Joseph McBride
320 pp., 64 pp. of illus.
80674-6 $14.95

FELLINI ON FELLINI
Federico Fellini
192 pp., 35 photos & film stills
80673-8 $13.95

HITCH
The Life and Times of
Alfred Hitchcock
John Russell Taylor
336 pp., 31 photos
80677-0 $14.95

BERGMAN ON BERGMAN
Interviews with Ingmar Bergman
Stig Björkman, Torsten Manns,
and Jonas Sima
288 pp., 328 film stills & photos
80520-0 $13.95

CHAPLIN
His Life and Art
David Robinson
896 pp., 185 illus.
80600-2 $21.95

THE CINEMA OF
ORSON WELLES
Peter Cowie
262 pp., 131 photos
80201-5 $14.95

COPPOLA
A Biography
Updated Edition
Peter Cowie
352 pp., 89 photos
80598-7 $14.95

THE DARK SIDE OF
THE SCREEN
Film Noir
Foster Hirsch
229 pp., 188 photos
80203-1 $16.95

EXPERIMENTAL ANIMATION
Origins of a New Art
Robert Russett and Cecile Starr
224 pp., 300 illus.
80314-3 $14.95

FILM AS FILM
Understanding and Judging Movies
V. F. Perkins
New introd. by Foster Hirsch
204 pp.
80541-3 $12.95

THE FILMS IN MY LIFE
François Truffaut
368 pp.
80599-5 $14.95

THE FLEISCHER STORY
Revised Edition
Leslie Cabarga
192 pp., over 300 illus.
80313-5 $16.95

FRITZ LANG
Lotte Eisner
420 pp., 162 photos
80271-6 $14.95